PRAISE F~~~~
BEFORE ALL IS SAI~~

"When you want the best advice, you ~~~~ ~~~~ people you know. Pat Miles is one of those people, and her story puts her in a unique position to offer honest, practical, and compassionate advice. This book is a blessing for survivors navigating the toughest days of their lives."

—Harvey Mackay,
NYT #1 Bestselling Author of
Swim With the Sharks Without Being Eaten Alive

"For a culture that finds it difficult to talk about the end of life, *Before All is Said and Done* is the roadmap we all need to navigate the practicalities of death while experiencing shock, loss, and grief."

—Lee Woodruff,
NYT Bestselling Author

"As a former lawyer and judge, I had neither thought about nor been intimidated by end-of-life financial issues. But *Before All is Said and Done* paints vividly the difficult realities my wife could encounter should I pass first. The book's read, and the understandably difficult discussions with your spouse and others, are musts for married couples."

—Rick Solum,
Retired Hennepin County Judge

"Preparing for and navigating the wealth management challenges of losing a spouse is a critically important topic not adequately addressed by the financial industry. Pat Miles does us all a service in tackling this head-on in her honest, moving, and compelling personal narrative."

—John Taft,
Vice Chair of Baird and Author of *Stewardship: Lessons Learned from the Lost Culture of Wall Street* and *A Force for Good: How Enlightened Finance Can Restore Faith in Capitalism*

"Through Pat's personal experience with many of these issues, she has compiled an extremely insightful and empathic view of the role of the caregiver. I think this is a must-read for persons and families with loved ones experiencing cognitive challenges."

—**Ronald Petersen,**
PhD, MD, Mayo Clinic Alzheimer's Disease Research Center
and the Mayo Clinic Study of Aging

Before All Is Said and Done

Practical Advice on Living and Dying Well

PAT MILES ZIMMERMAN with
SUZANNE SPARROW WATSON

Made for Success Publishing
P.O. Box 1775 Issaquah, WA 98027
www.MadeForSuccessPublishing.com

Distributed by Made for Success Publishing

First Printing

Library of Congress Cataloging-in-Publication data

Zimmerman, Pat Miles and Watson, Suzanne
    BEFORE ALL IS SAID AND DONE: Practical Advice on
    Living and Dying Well

p. cm.

LCCN: 2022914422
ISBN: 978-1-64146-747-6 (*Paperback*)
ISBN: 978-1-64146-748-3 (*eBook*)
ISBN: 978-1-64146-749-0 (*Audiobook*)

Printed in the United States of America

For further information contact Made for Success Publishing
+14255266480 or email service@madeforsuccess.net

CONTENTS

INTRODUCTION:
THE WIDOW'S WEB

WHEN AN ONCOLOGIST told my husband, Charles "Bucky" Zimmerman, that he had advanced and incurable cancer, the doctor's advice was to go home and get our affairs in order. I thought our affairs were in order. We had a will and trust, and Bucky, who was already on a path to retirement, had a partnership agreement with his firm that would provide for a comfortable future.

In our minds, we were set for life. But as it turned out, we were not set for death.

I first met Bucky in the early seventies. I was a news anchor at major network television stations in Minneapolis, and he was an up-and-coming attorney. Those were heady days; we were madly in love and enjoyed being a power couple as our careers soared. Bucky founded a law firm in Minneapolis and built it into a national powerhouse. In addition to news anchoring, I hosted a radio show and later developed a series of TV documentaries focused on notable Minnesotans called *A Pat Miles Special*.

After a few years of dating, our personal goals began to diverge. Although Bucky and I cared for each other deeply, our differences were too much to overcome, and we parted ways. Within a few years, we both married other people, and while Bucky did not have children, I was blessed with two daughters, Kate and Betsy.

Fast forward to 2005 when our paths crossed again. Luckily, we were both single, and our relationship rekindled as if no time had passed. We cherished our second chance and resolved not to lose one another; we were married in Santa Fe in 2006. I felt so fortunate, partnered with a man I admired and with whom I shared so many memories. I retired from the news station in Minneapolis, and we split our time between Minnesota and Arizona. Life was one adventure after another: travel, socializing, and appreciating our good fortune. Then, almost overnight, everything changed.

In November 2018, we were on a cruise with my two daughters when something seemed different. Bucky was tired. He slept all the time. This was not the man I knew, the man who could not sit still for even a moment and was always planning the next activity. As a young man, he played against tennis icon Arthur Ashe in the US Open Tennis Championship. At the age of seventy-two, he still had athletic prowess; he exercised every day, had a thirty-two-inch waist, and prided himself on his healthy lifestyle.

I attributed Bucky's fatigue to his relentless work schedule. His law firm had become the go-to firm for successful big class-action suits, including the tobacco and NFL concussion cases, so his workload was never-ending. But even after we returned home from that relaxing vacation, he remained weak and fatigued.

We realized that something was not right, so we went to the emergency room at the Mayo Clinic in Scottsdale, Arizona. One hour later, Bucky was diagnosed with stage four pancreatic cancer.

Bucky succumbed to the cancer on February 24, 2019.

I am sure his death was caused by a blood clot triggered by the cancer. I was trying to nap when the end came. There was not even a minute left for me to jump off the bed and reach Bucky's side before he took his last breath. My daughter, Kate, was reading a poem to him when he became agitated. She called my name and said there was something wrong.

In an instant, it was over. To say I was not prepared would be an understatement. It was a shock in so many ways, both the suddenness and the finality.

Since then, I have made mistake after mistake in dealing with the aftermath of Bucky's death. I have made financial and emotional blunders. I hired the wrong professionals and then lacked the will to fire them. I have spent countless nights lying awake with worry—and thousands of dollars on useless or plain bad advice from people who saw me as easy prey.

I was not reluctant or afraid to ask for help and advice. But the truth is, there is not much out there that helped me face the practical challenges I encountered. Yes, there are many books written for widows, but most of them focus on grief. Many of them are authored by a woman about her singular experience.

I also found that while I could Google "probate" and "right of survivorship," I could not Google "how to be a widow for dummies." There was nothing that answered all the questions I had to face. If you have recently lost a partner, you may be faced with the same problems.

That is why I wrote this book. This is not the book I expected to write or the story I expected to tell. As a journalist and reporter who worked for thirty years in radio and television, I have great tales about the people I interviewed and the places I visited. I planned to someday write a book about those experiences. But as the saying goes, "We plan, God laughs," and I learned firsthand that life is full of the unexpected.

While I didn't foresee writing this book, I began to realize that I was not alone in what I envision as the "widow's web"—a place where I have felt frozen and unable to escape. I realized that the tragic turn in my life was not only an opportunity to fulfill my dream of writing a book, but to help others at the same time.

I found that many widows who are in a position to offer good advice are just not talking. It occurred to me that they were not talking because no one was asking. So, I began my research for this book by interviewing other widows and found that although their circumstances differed, there was also a common theme: There's not much pragmatic advice out there from those who have traveled this road.

I have interviewed widows of all ages and from every walk of life, and I believe their compelling stories and advice will help others avoid many of the pitfalls of widowhood. Some have lost their homes and family relationships. Others have faced companies that refuse to pay them accrued retirement benefits. Many spoke about professionals billing for work never done. They also spoke eloquently and truthfully about grief, loss, and life alone.

I also interviewed accountants, estate planning attorneys, physicians, grief counselors, and a myriad of others who supplied insight into the sometimes-overwhelming world of the newly widowed. They provided realistic advice based on years of helping clients.

This book is for anyone who is currently trying to navigate the challenge of widowhood. But it is also for anyone in a relationship, who I implore to read this well before death comes knocking at their door. I believe that this book can help others avoid the mistakes and pitfalls encountered by so many newly widowed people.

I hope the sage advice from experts and the stories from surviving spouses will provide comfort and a plan of action.

Pat Miles Zimmerman

CHAPTER ONE:
GOING THROUGH HELL
The Grim Fog of Grief

"WHAT HURTS THE MOST WAS BEING SO CLOSE."
Rascal Flatts

A FTER BUCKY DIED and the funeral was over, I found myself lost. Lost in paperwork and responsibilities, but mostly lost in grief and depression. There was so much coming my way from so many different directions, and I was in no state to deal with any of it. I should not have been making important decisions or signing legal documents, but I had no choice. I plowed ahead, doing what others advised me to do, with little comprehension of the ramifications.

I came to think of it as "the fog of grief," a time when I simply existed, hurting beyond measure, just trying to get through the day. Of course, I knew then that I was not alone in my feelings of loss, but in researching this book, it was confirmed: Every person I spoke with experienced the same fog.

This was not a subject I knew anything about, but when the fog began to consume me and affect every facet of my life, it became my mission to better understand the process of grief and how to manage it. I learned there are many phases associated with grief: anger, guilt, sadness, pain, disillusionment. Most people go through at least some of those phases. We get so tied into holding on to life as we knew it. When someone loses their spouse, they often deny their new reality. They think, "This isn't me; this isn't my life." But it is.

GRIEF: LEARNING TO LIVE IN A WORLD OF TREMENDOUS SADNESS

I wanted to speak with professional therapists and counselors about how to handle grief, but the first person I wanted to talk to was Nancy, a good friend who is also a widow. I met Nancy and her husband forty years ago when I moved to Minneapolis. They were a dynamic couple who both had jobs in television news. They seemed to share everything in common and were the kind of couple who could finish each other's sentences.

When Bill died of cancer several years ago, so did a big part of Nancy. She became unrecognizable to me. She gained weight, suffered from depression, and lost her amazing zest for life. Years went by before the "old" Nancy began to reappear. I didn't have any idea what Nancy had suffered until I lost my own husband.

I felt terrible that I had not known how to help her or even talk to her about Bill's death. But when Bucky got sick, she was the first person I called. She was the person who knew what to say and how to say it to me. Nancy is full of wisdom about grief and how to live with it, all lessons learned the hard way.

Nancy was seventeen years old when she met Bill at a party. At the time, he was working at a local television station, and Nancy aspired to do the same. They formed a friendship that eventually turned into a thirty-eight-year marriage. They both became local television celebrities in their hometown, Minneapolis.

Nancy experienced many challenges after Bill died. Amid all of her issues, including financial and legal problems, her foremost challenge was her grief. She was daunted by the prospect of finding her footing and building a new life. Nancy has always been an enterprising person, someone who worked efficiently and reveled in the instant gratification of accomplishing a task. But she learned in therapy that working through grief takes time. Her therapist told Nancy that as much as she wanted her pain to stop, there was no quick fix.

With her typical determination, Nancy embarked on a mission to work through her grief. She decided that if she hurt, she would hurt; if she wanted to cry, she would cry. She acknowledged that the only way to reach the other side of grief was to experience it fully. While some of her friends had assumed a stiff upper lip attitude after losing a spouse, Nancy knew that would not make her better. "It's a road full of pain and agony," she said, "but you have to walk it. If you can embrace that, and if you know you can live through it, there will be a day when it feels different."

Nancy found that the adage "grief will be better in time" was a myth. She kept waiting for the hurt to hurt a little less, but it never let up. She finally decided to stop waiting for it to go away. "I must agree to live with it, and if I live with it, then it can sit over there in the corner. I find myself saying to the grief, 'Don't interfere with every second of my life, but I understand you're going to live there. I cannot wish you out of the house.'"

After my conversation with Nancy, I turned to four professionals to gain a better understanding of how to move through grief.

Lynn Kiely has spent forty-five years as a psychotherapist, focusing on helping people use their strengths and resources to find workable solutions and a deeper understanding of themselves.

Anne Murphy is a community death educator who specializes in thanatology, the scientific study of death and the practices associated with it, from the practical to the spiritual.

Anne Gettle is a clinical social worker for Essentia Health in Duluth, Minnesota. In Anne's practice, she specializes in helping clients work through the emotions associated with the loss of a loved one.

I also sought the counsel of Michele Neff-Hernandez. Michele is the co-founder of Soaring Spirits. She was widowed at the age of thirty-five when a car struck her husband while he was on his evening bike ride. He died instantly. She struggled with finding practical information for women who had been widowed, so she began to ask questions of other women who had also lost their husbands. Her connection with these women led her to establish Soaring Spirits International in 2008 with a friend who was also a recent widow. They organize weekend gatherings for widowed people called Camp Widow, which are a combination of retreat, conference, and gathering of friends.

THERE IS NO TIMELINE FOR GRIEF

Lynn Kiely started our conversation by explaining that grief can be overwhelming. The trauma of a loved one being there one moment and not there the next is enormous. There is a disbelief that the death has occurred, and a numbness sets in. She mentioned that she has seen this even with clients whose spouses had been ill for years. Lynn believes the age-old advice to not make any big decisions for a year after the death of a spouse is wise because newly widowed people are not thinking fully or clearly.

For example, Lynn told me that a client's husband was diagnosed with dementia. He also had a pacemaker, and when the time came to replace its battery, he declined. He knew the decision would eventually kill him, but he did not want to be dependent on his wife or have his medical condition ruin her life. She eventually agreed with and respected her husband's decision. After he died, Lynn's client was in a mental fog. It was as if she was disassociated from herself, with her thinking completely muddled. She admitted that she had made a lot of bad decisions over the previous few months due to "the fog." This was someone you might reasonably conclude would not go through that fog, given that she and her husband knew for months that he would die, but she still went through it.

Lynn helped me better understand the complexities of grief. She views grief as a normal part of processing, managing, and coping with loss. She told me some people grieve internally, while others openly express more emotion. Some people experience some measure of post-traumatic stress disorder (PTSD). For some, it is helpful to write down how they feel, and for others, journaling is the last thing they want to do. Some people put up pictures; others want to put away everything that reminds them of the person who just died. The important thing is to understand that everyone must grieve in their own way.

Anne Gettle told me her clients experience similar reactions to the loss of a partner. She emphasized that there is no timeline for grief; it's more about what people do with the time. She's worked with women who lost their husbands five years ago but have never allowed themselves to feel their grief.

She talked about how some people bury themselves in work or parenting. When you are parenting small children, there is no time to wallow in grief; you have to make sure that everyone has socks and shoes in the morning. The demands of everyday life can delay dealing with grief.

Some widows say that after they experienced all of the first anniversaries and milestones in the year after their partner died, the worst of their pain was over. But some widows say that the second year of widowhood was worse than the first. Anne said that many times, widows do not feel better after the first year because they spent that time dealing with complicated issues, such as administering a trust or will, dividing up personal effects, or dealing with emotional family problems. These issues often affect a person's ability to process their grief and begin to reimagine their life.

In fact, Anne mentioned that she has some clients who decide to stay stuck in their grief. They say, "This is where I live now." Ten years later, when they hear their dead spouse's name, they still cry. Living with such constant grief is difficult, but unfortunately, many people do so if they don't have the capacity or the support to walk through their grief.

Anne has also seen the opposite problem to sitting in grief—people who want to run through it too quickly. There is no short-cut, no cheat code for it. She has seen people intensely grieving over something insignificant a few years down the line because they haven't done the deep, slow walk through the real source of their grief.

Lynn and I spoke about the depression that can set in after the death of a spouse. Lynn emphasized that it is important that people understand the basic difference between grief and depression. For instance, when a woman has postpartum depression, people can make the mistake of thinking, "Oh, this is just part of giving birth." They believe that it is just a phase. Lynn acknowledged that sometimes it is depression—but sometimes it is not. She said that if people do not have the construct and context to understand what is going on with them, they can just slip deeper and deeper into depression.

Lynn explained the differences between grief and depression. She told me depression is often more biochemical, or sometimes brought on by situations. One could see grief as a situational depression, but it is important to define it differently. That's because grief is a normal response to loss, even though it has some similarities to some symptoms of depression, such as fatigue, difficulty making decisions, or disinterest.

One of the things Lynn said that resonated with me was that it is common to go through a phase where you can feel crazy. It is natural to think, "What is going on with me, and when is this going to end?" Lynn mentioned clients who questioned their own mental stability. That is why she feels it is important to have people who understand you, accept you, and do not get frightened by these emotions. If you do not have people like that in your life, a therapist can be helpful in the process of grieving. And, if it is a good therapist, they can normalize the process.

Anne Murphy, the community death educator, began our conversation by explaining some of the realities of death. She told me that in death, there is something that clears the lens. We cannot turn away from this new reality, but it can be hard to acknowledge death, even with a terminal diagnosis. Physicians may urge ongoing treatments, or the dying person may not want to discuss the diagnosis or their death. Because grief is unique, the process is different for every person. You grieve what you love, so if you are in deep grief, it is just a response to the love you had for the person who died. It will always be with you, and it is a part of who you are.

Anne believes that the way *not* to deal with grief is to ignore it. She urges her clients to "surrender sooner" because the sooner they address it, the better it will be for them. It is important to their overall health and well-being to be a participant in their grief. There must be a place where they can let go of their grief, whether that is a grief group, meditation, therapy, or church, whatever works best for them.

If they are not speaking about their grief, or not dealing with it in an active way, the grief will not go away. She observes, "That is the sticky wicket about emotions. They will find their way out, and there needs to be something that supports that movement and that motion."

When Anne talked about surrendering sooner, I thought about my friend, Nancy, who told me she has come to realize that for the rest of her life, the grief of Bill's absence is going to live in that metaphorical corner. Once she accepted that, she began to work around it and stopped waiting for it to dissipate. Today she says, "People tell you it is going to go away, and you want to believe that. It does not go away, but it does get different. You figure out a way to live with it."

HOW DO YOU FIND A WAY FORWARD?

I asked Anne Gettle for her guidance on how to move forward after a death. She told me that finding a new way forward is really hard but you never know what will grow from the seeds you plant. You never know what will come from going to that conference because your therapist said you should. You never know what will come from taking a walk.

Anne asks her clients, "What are you doing to take care of yourself?" She isn't alluding to everyday tasks like balancing the checkbook, cleaning the bathroom, or folding laundry. Her intent is to have clients think about what will make them feel good. She encourages them to find something meaningful in each day. She told me that when you lose someone, the meaning can fall out of your life. The challenge is to find a new normal and a new meaning.

My friend Bonnie felt as if a lifetime of memories had been altered when her husband, Dan, died. As a new widow, I paid attention to other widows and assumed they were coping much better than I was. Bonnie was one of those people. To me, Bonnie seemed to be doing great. She wasn't. Bonnie said she could function, doing the everyday things she needed to keep the household running, but the emotional change was hard to grasp.

Bonnie and Dan physically looked like a mismatched couple; she stood barely over five feet while he towered over her by more than a foot. But as different as they were physically, they were a perfect match by any other standard. They both had outgoing personalities, a love of sport, and a devotion to family. Uniquely, they had one other similarity: shared childhood memories. Dan's family moved across the street from Bonnie when she was just eight years old. They became fast friends at once, and on Bonnie's sixteenth birthday, when she finally had permission to date, they began a lifelong love affair. They were married in their early twenties and were soon living what she describes as the American dream: a nice house, successful career, two children, and a plethora of friends.

Their idyllic married life continued for forty years until it was brutally interrupted by Dan's diagnosis of metastatic prostate cancer. Dan sought treatment over the course of several years but, ultimately, the cancer prevailed.

The longevity of their relationship made Bonnie's adjustment to widowhood especially difficult. She explained, "I don't have many memories of when he wasn't in my life. We grew up together, so I do not know how to not have him in my life. He is my whole past." Eating was especially difficult. She realized that meals—the discussion of menus, cooking together, hosting dinners—were a very social activity. After Dan died, she ate to subsist, but her zest for meals was gone.

Bonnie kept busy by dining out, golfing, and exercising at the gym, but her constant activity became a two-edged sword. Like me, other people saw her being active and assumed she was fine. But she was not fine. She was "lonely as hell," she said, but no one ever saw that; no one saw that she was just trying to fill a big void. To add to her sorrow, her faithful dog, Riley, died soon after Dan.

Suddenly, everything that brought her comfort was gone. She felt untethered. Bonnie worked hard to stay occupied, but the harder she tried, the more exhausted she became. As she describes it, she was "flapping in the wind."

Even Bonnie's relationship with her children changed after Dan died. Dan had warned Bonnie that their children would not fill the void he would leave; they had busy lives and did not live nearby. Dan had been right. As with many families, the children had perceived Dan and Bonnie as one parental unit, not as individual people, and they were struggling with their own grief. She observed, "They had a tough time thinking of me in the same way they always had. We all were grieving and in pain, and we had to work through it. We had to establish a new relationship for the future."

In addition to the change in relationship with her children, Bonnie experienced a change in her status within their social circle. I had learned from Lynn Kiely that it is common for newly widowed people to sometimes feel that if they are not part of a couple, they have no identity. That is especially true if the widow's former social life was exclusively limited to couples. Bonnie and Dan had an active social life with an array of friends before Dan's illness. But during the last few months of Dan's illness, she had a preview of the neglect to come. When all the treatment options were exhausted, and the outcome was clear, some of Dan's once good friends did not take time to visit. Most who did never returned. Bonnie was angered by this, but Dan encouraged her to let it go. They both decided to skip a funeral for him, concluding that the people who had cared about him most paid their respects while he was alive.

Once Dan was gone, Bonnie found herself living in a world of couples. Some friends they had socialized with for years no longer invited her to dinner parties. She went from being included in everything to feeling isolated. Her social network let her down, and that only added to her grief.

Within two years of Dan's death, an influx of new residents moved into Bonnie's community, and she formed new friendships. The new group never knew Dan, so they did not view Bonnie as Dan's widow. Today, she is active, has a new dog, Charlie, and is moving forward—and Dan, her lifelong friend and mate, is always with her in spirit. Bonnie is not in a hurry to enter into a new relationship. She feels that at some point, Dan will have a hand in putting the right person in her path.

Entering into a new relationship after the death of a spouse can be fraught with problems. Lynn Kiely said that many of her clients have an urge to dissipate some of their pain through the excitement of a new relationship. She has observed that men and women experience being suddenly single in different ways. Men move quickly to replace the person they lost. Women usually take a lot longer to enter a new relationship. But she said that while trying can help, moving on too quickly can be a mistake. She emphasized how important it is for people to take the time to find their own way, determine new life goals, and establish their new identity. Widowed people need to discover and pursue their passions in creating a new life.

Lynn counseled that one must go through the entire process of feeling the loss of a relationship and experience the emotional expansion that happens when going through a loss. Only when a person has re-stabilized their life and accepted their new situation can they enter a relationship in a positive way.

After Bucky died, I did not seek professional help to handle the emotional wreckage, which I now realize was a crucial mistake. I also did not join a grief group, which might have helped me realize that I was not alone in my grief journey and where I could have learned lessons from those who had already been down the path of widowhood.

Michele Neff-Hernandez offered advice about reaching out to other widowed people specifically as a way of processing grief. Michele's organization, Soaring Spirits, caters their grief support to the individual. She emphasized that the ability for a widow to connect with other widowed people is immensely powerful. For example, she mentioned that younger widows often feel out of place in grief groups in which everyone else is older. Conversely, older widows might not feel safe or comfortable using the internet, so they seek an in-person connection.

Soaring Spirits provides an array of choices, such as a 24/7 online community and regional get-togethers for those who want to meet in person. They also offer a one-on-one matching service to connect widows who can email each other for support. They have helped more than four million people, and the average age of their client is fifty-three. You will read more about Michele and Soaring Spirits in Chapter Seven, where she discusses how they supported widows during the COVID pandemic.

All of the professionals I spoke with helped me understand that you cannot go back to the life you used to have. It is difficult to reimagine a new life when you are in your seventies or eighties, but you have to go through the process of reimagining to get to a new, productive one. As Lynn Kiely told me, it might be a smaller life, and it might be a simpler life. Lynn offered her own ninety-five-year-old widowed mother as an example. Her life is quite simple. She gets pleasure from just reading, and at ninety-five years old, that is enough for her. She is still a very joyful person. She is fortunate that she has figured out how to rebuild her life, even with very few relationships.

As I was told over and over again, the nature of life is all about change. It is all about new beginnings and endings and everything in between. It is uncomfortable to be on an unknown path where we do not know where the end will be. The truth is we may not be able to see it or understand it until we are there.

LESSONS LEARNED ABOUT THE FOG OF GRIEF:

- Expect to feel numb after the loss of a partner.
- Don't make any big decisions for a year.
- Grieve in your own way; don't linger, but don't rush through it.
- Learn the difference between grief and depression.
- Engage a professional to help guide you through the grief process.
- Find support through family, friends, and/or community news.
- Surrender sooner and face the new reality.
- Find something meaningful in each day.
- Be creative and find your new identity.

CHAPTER TWO:
DON'T DIE BEFORE YOU'RE READY

The Need for Lawyers with a Moral Compass

"DON'T BEND, DON'T BREAK, BABY,
DON'T BACK DOWN."
Bon Jovi

S HORTLY AFTER BUCKY and I were married, he had to drag me to the estate attorney's office to execute our estate documents. I was so blissfully happy that the last thing on my mind was writing a will or trust, and besides that, I didn't really understand the intricacies of them. To me, these legal matters were best left for Bucky to figure out. I didn't want to think about them, and I didn't want to talk about them. Spending an hour in an attorney's office was akin to getting a tooth pulled. So I allowed Bucky to take the lead and signed whatever he placed in front of me.

The attorney Bucky hired to draw up our documents was a longtime friend of his. This attorney was older, in ill health, and probably not as up-to-date as he should have been in drafting and executing estate documents. The bigger problem turned out to be that this attorney had no loyalty, or any interest, in my affairs.

When I look back on my reaction to drawing up a will and trust, I wonder how or who could have convinced me how important it was to pay attention. Sometimes we learn the hard way. I learned that the aftermath of a death is not the time to begin the process of understanding legal documents.

When Bucky's illness advanced to end-stage, I arranged for hospice care and my friend, Nancy, to come stay with me. Because her husband had also died of cancer, she knew the signs that Bucky's death was imminent. She was also aware that our affairs were not in order. At her urging, I called a notary to the house so Bucky could execute changes to his will. Bucky died the day after he signed those papers.

I did not really know what he was signing or why. But I should have.

If not for Nancy, I would have spent thousands of dollars more in legal fees and lawsuits administering his estate. As it turned out, I had plenty of other legal issues that consumed my life over the next eighteen months.

In the days after Bucky's funeral, I began the task of sorting through his estate. First, I met with his law partners to go through his retirement benefits. Bucky had assured me I was entitled to them, as well as any of his outstanding billing for legal services. I expected things to go smoothly. After all, Bucky founded the firm and was responsible for the successful practice his partners enjoyed.

But the meeting was anything but smooth. The partners' position was that Bucky died before he officially retired; therefore, he was not a retiree of the firm. Consequently, I was not eligible to receive any of his retirement benefits. The financial security Bucky believed he left me was gone.

I was vulnerable and afraid without Bucky's guidance, but I was aware that I needed to hire an attorney to represent my interests. Just two weeks after Bucky's death, I was sitting at a conference table about to make the most crucial decision of my future: picking an estate attorney. I looked and acted like I knew what I was doing, but I had no idea.

I interviewed five lawyers, all handpicked by Bucky's bankers. I did not know any of them, but I trusted the bankers were referring people who would take diligent care of me. This is not the way things turned out. The estate attorney I selected accepted my case knowing he was resigning from his firm in a few weeks.

When he quit the law firm, no one bothered to tell me. The firm assigned my affairs to another attorney but failed to tell me for almost two months. That lack of introduction did not stop my new attorney from billing me and, as I later found out, charging me for work he never did. I had made a terrible mistake and then made it even worse by not firing this attorney and the law firm. I could not face the disruption or the confrontation it would involve. I did not ask for help or advice. I was too embarrassed to tell anyone what I had discovered.

If I could go back and do things differently following Bucky's death, I would have taken a good friend with me to every meeting I had. I'm not sure if it was arrogance or ignorance that made me believe I knew what I was doing or that people I placed my trust in knew what they were doing. I needed an extra set of eyes and ears that I didn't have, and I made some bad decisions as a result. I learned that you cannot think straight after the death of a spouse. You don't remember things, and you don't care about things. I would listen to people who were trying to help me and forget what they told me the next day.

I wish that Bucky and I had reviewed our estate documents before he died. Instead, we were consumed with his care, shuttling from one doctor's appointment to the next. We decided that his care was the only priority. We didn't worry about much else, and I guess I assumed everything else would be taken care of for me.

I learned that my situation was not unusual. In fact, it happens all too often when every "I" has not been dotted and "T" meticulously crossed. That is a difficult task under the best of circumstances and almost impossible when someone is sick and dying. Bucky and I were clinging to hope. Hope that he would get better and hope that he would live longer. Neither one of us was willing to talk about or acknowledge that he was dying and what that might mean for us. For me, to actually talk about death felt like "giving in" and "giving up," and I was not going to do that.

A big part of my reasons for writing this book is that I wanted to better understand how I could have handled things differently. The mistakes I made are not inevitable, but to avoid them requires hiring a trusted estate attorney to establish and administer legal documents in preparation for your own passing or the passing of your spouse. It also entails paying attention and being involved in understanding those documents.

I reached out to three estate attorneys, Susan Link, Maggie Green, and William Asp, to get their perspectives on how to best tackle the legal aspects of setting up a comprehensive estate plan. Susan Link has been an estate attorney for thirty-four years. She has helped hundreds of widows through the process of settling estates, going through probate (the official proving of a will), and dealing with the fallout of sorting through wills and trusts. Maggie Green founded Donohue Green Law Office in 2008 and manages legal matters that include preparing wills and trusts, as well as trust administration. William (Bill) Asp is an estate planning attorney with Best and Flanagan law firm. He works in the Private Wealth Planning division, focusing on estate and trust planning, administration, and litigation.

FINDING A TRUSTED PARTNER
TO HANDLE YOUR SPOUSE'S ESTATE

I spoke first with Maggie Green about the importance of having estate documents in place long before you need them.

Maggie told me one of the biggest problems she encounters in her practice is that people avoid writing their wills. She observes that there is a reluctance in our society to think or talk about dying. In addition, people do not want to meet with an attorney to talk about something they do not completely understand. In her experience, individuals need to be ready to talk about their own death and the need for a will before an attorney can be effective. She has observed that some people, even when facing a fatal diagnosis, still do not have the capacity to sit down and think through their estate plans.

I told Maggie about the young widows I spoke with whose husbands died without a will. Maggie said that is not unusual. She said many younger couples do not plan for death, which can leave minor children orphaned and without a guardian they would personally have chosen to care for their children. She said that these couples find it is just too difficult to even think about naming guardians, or they do not agree on who the guardians should be, so they get stuck and do nothing. The lack of named guardians can result in huge legal issues and discord among families.

All three attorneys I spoke with emphasized the importance of selecting a lawyer who can act as a trusted partner and who can communicate complex issues on a basic, understandable level. Bill Asp noted that oftentimes an estate attorney is the first attorney a widow has ever hired, and by the time she meets with that attorney, she is already mired in litigation because there was no estate plan or something has gone wrong within the family. That is not a situation in which anyone wants to find themselves.

Susan Link confirmed that the aftermath of a death is not the time to begin the process of understanding estate documents because there are often many underlying emotional issues involved when someone dies. She corroborated what I already knew—the partner left behind faces many tasks and a mountain of paperwork, and you only have so much capacity for conversations about the estate documents and issues related to the person who passed away when you are in the fog of grief.

Susan said that when someone is vulnerable, it is especially important that they work with a professional they are comfortable with and, optimally, someone they have worked with before. Much like choosing the right therapist to help process grief, widows need a good lawyer with a good moral compass and a center of gravity to guide them in their decision-making. According to Susan, estate planning should not be thought of as rocket science; in fact, she says it is very logical, and everyone is smart enough to understand the basics.

I told her that Bucky's bankers had selected the estate attorneys for me to interview. She related that is a common occurrence, and when that is the case, the surviving spouse should get references from people they know and trust. It is especially important that the attorney has a good history in implementing estate documents—not just drafting them.

Too often, Susan sees surviving spouses go back to the attorney who drafted the documents for their deceased partner, even if they have no prior relationship with that attorney. That means they are operating on blind faith that the attorney will execute everything correctly. She said that many people do not realize they can use their own attorney to administer the documents rather than hiring the same people who drafted them originally.

I mentioned to Susan that Bucky and I had not reviewed our estate documents together. She said that in her practice, she tells her estate planning clients, "I want both of you here" because she wants to be able to look both people in the eye to see if they comprehend what is being discussed. If she sees a *deer in the headlights* look, she backs up and goes through everything again.

HOW DO I SELECT SUCCESSOR TRUSTEES AND POWERS OF ATTORNEY?

After the legal trauma I experienced in finalizing Bucky's estate, I vowed that my daughters would not go through the hell I did when the time came to administer my estate. I began the work of getting my own estate documents in order. In addition to updating my trust, I knew I needed to declare who had powers of attorney for my health care and financial affairs. Susan explained to me that these are extremely important documents. She said, "Dying is big money. Health care, estate administration, tax returns, funeral costs, and memorials: all the things that occur when someone dies involve lots of money. That is why it is critical to have all of the estate documents in place well before you need them. That includes naming a successor trustee."

Susan told me that when an estate attorney drafts a trust, some people will name that lawyer as successor trustee, assuming that the lawyer will then be there to assist with the administration of the trust after they die. She said the same holds true for accountants, who some people choose to name as a successor trustee. But she cautions that once the lawyer or accountant is named on your legal documents, they will be involved after you die. Susan pointed out that if you name a family member or friend as successor trustee, they can use the lawyer or accountant you trusted, but they are not limited to using them. Successor trustees are free to use a firm of their choosing.

But how do you choose who your successor trustee should be? Susan's best advice is to name children as successor trustees. If someone does not have children, they should name another family member or a friend who they trust to act on their behalf.

In addition to a trust or will, two other essential documents need to be part of an estate plan: an advance directive for health care and the designation of a financial power of attorney.

Susan pointed out that one of the biggest drains on finances is the medical costs near the end of life. Consequently, she said everybody needs an advance directive, often called a health care directive, and they need to name a person who can speak for them if they are in a health care crisis.

Her recommendation is if you have more than one child, avoid giving each child equal authority in that advance directive. Only one child should be named, and then the next child as the successor if the first child is unable to perform their duties. The problem with naming multiple children is that if they do not agree on care, the doctor is not legally empowered to break the tie. Choosing one child over others can be extremely awkward, but this is the best thing for yourself and your family. Pick the child who you believe would make the same decisions as you. If possible, explain your reasoning to your other children to avoid conflict at a later date over why this child was selected.

I asked Susan if the same "one child" suggestion was also true for financial affairs. In fact, she told me, it is the opposite of the health care directive. She often advises clients to name more than one person on a financial power of attorney document, which grants those named the authority to act on their behalf in financial matters during their lifetime. If clients have more than one child, she tells them to name all of them and require that if they ever have to use the document, they all have to sign jointly. This co-signing will prevent one child from looking at another sideways, saying, "Did you take money out of that account?"

I discovered that it is a lot of work to think through and document all of your final wishes. It can also involve a lot of expense, depending on the complexity of the estate. I spoke with Bill Asp about that and he verified that some of his prospective clients are reluctant to spend the money necessary to establish sound estate documents. He acknowledged that there are a lot of expenses associated with dying, but he believes that those costs can be mitigated by some pre-planning. For example, he recommends pre-paying funeral expenses, setting up a revocable trust to avoid probate, and designating beneficiaries for every asset.

Bill explains to clients that are reluctant to spend money on estate documents that their options are to either put everything in writing or have their family fight in court for two years. When they weigh the two options, it becomes clear that a good estate plan ends up paying for itself a hundred times over.

Bill told me some people inquire about using online forms to write their will in order to save money. Again, he explains to them that using these generic forms usually backfires because the cost of fixing a will or trust written incorrectly is enormous. Trying to fix the problem after someone has already died is even more complicated. The surviving spouse is not usually someone who is experienced with legal documents, so he or she can get mired in decoding rules and statutes, which can be very confusing for a grieving spouse.

Maggie said she also advises clients that in addition to drawing up estate documents, they need to organize their financial accounts. She encourages clients to make a list of their accounts and include information on where to find key documents. She suggests that couples itemize their financial assets and next to every item, write down how it is titled and then have a column about how that asset will transfer upon death. These actions make the plan easier to administer when the time comes.

Maggie also recommends to clients that they leave instructions for their burial and memorial service. Finally, she stressed that it is critical to keep these documents and lists updated. She suggests setting up a regular interval on your calendar to review your legal and personal documents.

WHAT ABOUT THE DECEASED SPOUSE'S BUSINESS?

As I learned, there is another level of complexity to an estate when the deceased spouse was a business owner. I spoke with Bill about what happened to me with Bucky's business. He told me that disputes between business partners and a surviving spouse of a partner are all too common. Sometimes he said it stems from there being only a handshake deal in place versus legal documentation. Sometimes the business owner might not have a buy-sell agreement in place and that can make it a lot more expensive and time-consuming for the survivors to figure out what to do with the assets of the business.

Bill advises all business owners to have conversations with their family and with business partners about what will happen after the owner dies. He said a lot of lawsuits arise because there was no communication ahead of time and everyone ends up fighting about the business ownership or assets. I can certainly attest to that.

Shortly after I began my conversations with the estate attorneys, I met a friend for lunch and related my experiences with legal problems after Bucky died. She told me I needed to speak with her friend, Kim, whose husband died without any legal documents in place.

I was intrigued, so I arranged to speak with Kim by phone. Kim's husband, Rob, died of cancer that started as melanoma, then spread to his lymph nodes, and finally metastasized to his brain. Despite extensive treatments, eventually the tumors in his brain began to bleed, erasing his memory and personality. She asked the oncologist for an estimate on how long Rob might last. He said, "Weeks to months; get your affairs in order."

But there was no will or trust for Kim to get in order. They had intended to do a formal will earlier that year, but Rob was too sick, so they canceled the meeting with their attorney. Plus, whenever Rob suggested they discuss what Kim needed to know after his death, Kim would break down in tears, so they kept putting it off.

Still, Kim thought she had Rob's wishes in hand. Two years earlier, before a trip to Israel, Kim mentioned to Rob that if something should happen to them, it would be problematic because they did not have wills in place. So, Rob wrote on a piece of paper, "I leave everything to my loving wife." A few months before Rob's decline, as they embarked on another trip, Rob again wrote a note saying, "I leave everything to my loving wife."

Kim felt secure, knowing she had two handwritten notes with Rob's signature, written two years apart, saying he was leaving everything to her. Unfortunately, they did not know that for the courts to legally recognize a handwritten will, it has to be witnessed by two additional people.

When Rob learned his cancer had metastasized, he did not want to hear anything negative. He did not want to hear anybody suggest that he was going to die; his intention was to live at least another two years, then make it to five. But he was already suffering the effects of his illness. He was on mega steroids and had become violent; his normal personality was altered. Rob was slipping away, and Kim was flailing.

That is when Rob's brother stepped in to assist her. He worked as a financial advisor, and although he had not come to visit them in over ten years, Kim gratefully accepted his offer to manage her finances. She appreciated the gesture; Rob was becoming increasingly difficult to care for, and she needed to devote more time to him.

Kim gave Rob's brother all their financial statements. Once he had reviewed everything, he asked Kim if Rob had a will. Kim showed him the two hand-written notes, where Rob left everything to her. His brother looked at them and said, "Well, I've got to believe he wants to leave something to the family." Kim was baffled by Rob's statement. She told him, "I'm his family."

A month later, Rob's brain hemorrhaged. The doctor convened the family and told them Rob was no longer capable of making any decisions. The doctor appointed Kim as Rob's advocate.

Kim began by filing paperwork with Rob's company. They asked her for Rob's Social Security number. Not only did she not know it, but she did not even know where to find it. She thought Rob was lucid enough to ask him about it, but his response was, "I don't know what a Social Security number is."

Rob's brother stepped in, but by then some red flags had been raised for Kim about his involvement. He was communicating with

Rob by drawing stick figures, representing himself, Rob's other brother, his niece and nephew, and Kim. Using the figures, Rob's brother asked Rob to designate him and Rob's other brother as the beneficiaries of his 401(k). He drew up an irrevocable trust with the two brothers as beneficiaries and put Rob and Kim's Cape Cod beach house in it. Under the brother's plan, the only asset Kim would receive was Rob's life insurance, which would barely cover the huge mortgage on their primary home.

Kim was alarmed by her brother-in-law's actions. She knew she needed Rob to legalize the wishes he wrote on the two scraps of paper, regardless of the doctor's assessment of his mental condition. Rob had a friend who was an attorney, so she asked him to visit Rob and draw up a will.

The attorney told Rob he would have to prove that he was of sound mind and body before signing a legal document. Clearly the attorney knew Rob was not able to make decisions, but he proceeded to draw up documents anyway. Rob left 10 percent of his 401(k) to each of his brothers and a smaller amount to his niece and nephew. The rest of the estate was left to Kim.

Kim was not happy that Rob's family was receiving anything. They had not been in touch for over ten years and had only shown an interest in Rob when he was dying. But Kim decided that she did not want to argue with Rob about money in the last days of his life.

The cancer finally took Rob's life. His funeral took place on Kim's 50th birthday. Shortly afterward, Kim's legal problems began. Rob's brothers contested the will Rob signed during those last few days of his life. Kim had sold the Cape Cod house after Rob died, and the brothers took issue with that as well. Rob's brothers and Kim ended up counter-suing each other, and the proceedings dragged on for five years. After long months of negotiation, they finally settled their dispute. Kim received Rob's 401(k) money and the life insurance. But she had to pay Rob's brothers $110,000 in cash. Kim ended up with less than $12,000 after paying her debts, attorneys' fees, and Rob's brothers. Kim has not spoken to Rob's brothers since.

Looking back, Kim acknowledges that she did not have good legal advice, and the lack of formal documents hurt her both financially and emotionally. Kim advises everyone to prepare a will, and to do so before their spouse is ill, when relatives can come out of the woodwork.

Kim's situation seemed unusual to me, but when I spoke with the estate attorneys, they told me these type of family problems are actually quite common. Susan, Maggie, and Bill all spoke about the importance of thinking through the implications of an estate plan on family members. They stress to their clients that both partners need to be comfortable with how their estate will be distributed. I learned from all three of them that when one spouse dies, the surviving spouse cannot change trusts or wills without going to court. If they do go to court to make changes, any of the other beneficiaries (such as children, stepchildren, or siblings) may disagree with the suggested changes, which means the court proceeding will turn into contested litigation. A contested litigation is both stressful and expensive.

In one respect I was very fortunate in settling Bucky's estate and establishing my own – my two daughters get along well and since Bucky did not have children, I was not dealing with a blended family. I had learned from many friends that the relationship between stepparent and stepchild can become frayed after the birth parent dies. I have devoted Chapter Four to that specific issue.

WHAT TO TELL THE CHILDREN
ABOUT YOUR ESTATE

When I spoke with Maggie, she emphasized the importance of communication with beneficiaries about your wishes for the distribution and division of your estate. She observed that a lot of problems arise when children do not know what the estate plan lays out. This can be especially true with blended families, but she sees it with all families. Children get upset that they did not know what the plan was, why things were set up the way they were, and why there is a trust involved.

Maggie is realistic about encountering problems after a death in the family. She told me, "Let's face it; sometimes people will find a way to create a problem. Oftentimes, survivors' reactions come down to personality and family history, and those are the things you cannot always plan around."

Maggie advises her clients that if they are comfortable, they should share their plan with their adult children, including how the estate will be distributed and who is named the co-trustees. That is most important if one of their children will be taking a leadership role in administering the trust and estate.

In my conversation with Bill, he echoed Maggie's observation about money sometimes tearing families apart. He told me, "It is common for people to tell me, 'It's not about the money.' But an experienced mediator once told me, 'It's always about the money.' Money does funny things to people. A lot of times, the problems stem from long-term family grudges, and it all comes out after the death of a family member."

Bill explained to me that the litigation process in these circumstances is exceedingly difficult because it is both financial and emotional. It is not just what happens with the assets; it is what happens with the family. If a family sits in court for two years arguing with one another, that is detrimental to the family moving forward. Bill has seen family relationships damaged for life. In those cases, he said people are not only dealing with the death of a loved one, but the death of a family.

Bill encourages his clients to sit down with their children and talk through the estate plan; he said this is especially important in second marriages with blended families. He told me that some of his clients are not comfortable talking with their children about what they will inherit, but his experience is that the ones who do eliminate a lot of problems after their death.

He counseled that when things do go wrong, courts don't deal in *he said-she said* issues. They deal only in facts and what has been written down. It is much more difficult to overturn something in writing, as opposed to hearsay about what the deceased told someone.

Bill said the worst scenarios in court are when two family members disagree about what the deceased wanted. He said he hears a lot of "Dad said X" while a sibling says, "Dad said Y." The families actually dwindle the estate by spending tens or hundreds of thousands of dollars in legal fees fighting over who gets what.

Still, Bill has had clients in the middle of a family squabble who want to pursue litigation. In those cases, he lays out what they can expect from the legal process. A lot of these people have never litigated anything, so they can have unrealistic expectations about the amount of money at stake or the possibly detrimental effects of a prolonged litigation. He warns them that it can be a very lengthy and expensive process. He cautions them that it is never good when they end up arguing with each other in front of a judge.

And, he said, the fact is, no one wins. Often, from a financial standpoint, the best solution is to settle the case before it goes to court. Despite that, some clients will only be satisfied by making their case in front of a judge. The legal fees associated with a court case are so substantial that often people end up paying their attorneys a sizeable portion of what they would have inherited.

FIGHTING OVER GRANDMA'S PIE PLATE

In Maggie's experience, the amount of money in an estate does not necessarily correlate to how much arguing ensues or how difficult siblings make it for the one who is the executor. She said, "There is a joke among estate attorneys that everyone fights over grandma's pie plate."

Attorneys who work with these families know that they are not really fighting over the pie plate. Instead, they are falling back on old arguments and tensions within the family. Maggie allowed that sometimes she will have a family that really does want to fight about the pie plate—and they usually end up with litigation attorneys. Maggie encourages her clients to think about items in their estate that might have sentimental value to their heirs, such as jewelry or watches, household items, or even a set of golf clubs. She asks them to make a list of the items and, next to each one, designate who they want to receive it after their death.

I was fortunate that I did not have to fight extensive family battles in court. But I still encountered problems due to my lack of understanding of the legal process, and I suffered the consequences of lawyers taking advantage of that fact. I was consumed with grief after Bucky died and did what people told me to do, with little knowledge about what I was doing.

MY SPOUSE DIED. NOW WHAT?

Susan told me that when she is meeting with a newly widowed person, she advises them to do what I did not do—ask questions. She says if people are sitting in a meeting and are not sure what is being said or what the documents are supposed to be doing, they need to take the time to understand what is going on. Stop the discussion and ask questions! Her goal is to have informed, knowledgeable clients. She never wants a surviving spouse to be in a position where they look back and say, "I really had no idea what was going on."

Oftentimes after the death of a spouse, when estate documents are in place, an attorney handles all of the paperwork, and the court system is not involved. But, for various reasons, some estates end up in probate. Susan has found that some clients are not familiar with the probate process, and some of those who have heard of it are intimidated by the prospect. According to Susan, probate is not a big, nasty thing; it is simply a court-administered proceeding that appoints someone to act on behalf of their estate (a personal representative) and facilitates the distribution of assets based on a person's will, or the intestacy (dying without a valid will) laws if there is no will in place. Lawyers no longer go to court for this process; they file documents electronically. Susan reassures people entering into probate that it is not something to be afraid of; it simply puts structure around the administration of someone's assets.

Sometimes, problems arise when working with a law firm. That was certainly true in my case. I felt duped when I discovered the billing errors and inaccuracies from my attorney. Susan told me that while it isn't common, it does happen, and that clients need to carefully review all invoices before they issue payment. She also sees the opposite problem: widows who think everyone is out to take advantage of them. She told me that as a professional, it can be hard to deal with a skeptical client when she is trying to give good advice. That mindset is also more stressful for the client. That is another reason she encourages everyone to find an attorney they trust and, ideally, to locate that person in advance of actually needing to employ their services.

I related to Susan that I have friends who never had the responsibility for handling finances and are uncomfortable and unfamiliar with how to do it. These women have all of their household bills sent to their attorney for payment. Susan said having a law firm pay your bills can be a mistake. Not only is it an expensive way to pay bills, but it can also lock your heirs into using that law firm to settle your estate when the time comes. In addition, it leaves partners in the dark about what the bills are, their payment dates, and other logistics.

I learned so many lessons the hard way when it came to settling Bucky's estate. In hindsight, we should have had more discussions and thought through what would happen when one of us died. My hope is that the information provided in this chapter will help others avoid the pitfalls I encountered.

LESSONS LEARNED ABOUT ESTATE PLANNING:

- Have estate plan discussions and legal documents drawn up while both partners are alive and of sound mind. Ask questions of the professionals you work with until you are satisfied you understand them.

- Choose an estate attorney who can be a trusted advisor. If you don't know of one, ask friends for recommendations.

- Designate a family member as your successor trustee.

- Designate one person on your advance health care directive.

- Designate multiple people on your financial documents.

- Make a list of financial accounts and personal items, including where they can be found and who is to inherit what.

- Business owners should have documents that clearly spell out what should happen to the business upon their death.

CHAPTER THREE:
WHY DO I FEEL SO POOR?
The Benefit of Truly Trusted Financial Pros

"MONEY CHANGES EVERYTHING."
Cyndi Lauper

MONEY WAS THE one thing I believed I would not have to worry about after my husband, Bucky, died. Bucky had assured me that the retirement benefits from the law firm he founded and worked at for forty-seven years would take care of me for the rest of my life.

But he had been too optimistic. You may have heard the Bible verse, "For the love of money is the root of all evil." After Bucky's death, I learned firsthand that money can destroy our social values, ruin relationships, and wreak havoc in families and businesses.

I have learned this happens all the time to surviving spouses. Some surviving spouses did not have an expert to rely on, and still, others received inept advice. For me, I trusted people I should not have, and it cost me dearly. Unfortunately, my experience was not unique.

My friend Katie had an experience comparable to mine when her husband died. I first met Katie when she began dating Chip, one of Bucky's oldest friends. Chip and Katie met on a blind date set up by mutual friends. They both had children from previous marriages, and they dated almost three years before deciding to give marriage another try. For eight years, life together was idyllic.

There was a small medical hiccup the first year of their marriage. Chip was diagnosed with a tiny melanoma on his thigh, but the spot was removed, and he was declared cancer-free. They did not give it a second thought until four years later, when the cancer came back. This time it had metastasized to his liver and his diagnosis was terminal.

Chip, along with two partners, was the founder of an investment banking firm. He was a keen businessperson who had accumulated pensions and savings. But in the end, Chip's business partners threw his survivors under the bus.

After Chip died, the partners sold the company to a bigger investment banking firm. They cashed out for millions of dollars, but Chip's family was left out of the deal. Chip's partners determined that Chip's family got nothing because he died before he formally retired.

Chip's attorney filed a claim on behalf of the family and got a little money, but it was a pittance compared to what the others received. Katie was so overwhelmed with grief that she did not have the energy to fight for more. Looking back, she wishes that she had, so his family would have received what the other partners got for their families.

"Timing is everything," she told me. "The last thing you want to do when you are grieving is fight. So, I gave in."

Timing is indeed everything. When I told a friend I was researching the financial aspects of losing a partner, she recommended that I speak with Pam, a young widow who lost her husband during the COVID-19 pandemic. You will read more about their battles with the virus in Chapter Seven.

Pam and her husband, Martin, were a young couple living an enviable life. Pam, thirty-seven years old, and Martin, forty-two, were parents to two small children, a two-year-old and a four-month-old. Pam and Martin talked about writing wills and powers of attorney, but their busy schedules kept getting in the way. Martin worked as a speech pathologist in a hospital, and in his work, he saw young people die. At times he told Pam they should write wills, saying, "Tomorrow is never promised." But Pam could not foresee the need—they were both too young to focus on "death documents."

Enter the COVID-19 pandemic. Martin became one of the first victims of the virus in his town and died in March 2020. When Martin became fatally ill, the couple's lack of planning and documentation became a major obstacle for Pam.

As Pam said, she was left with "a lot to sort out." Everyday tasks that had once been routine suddenly became a nightmare. Beyond the normal legal aspects of settling an estate, her financial life became complex and expensive to sort through.

For example, Pam wanted to move Martin's credit cards into his iCloud account so nothing would get overlooked, but she did not have the password to his Apple account. She told me, "I began to think of these things when he was in the hospital, but what was I supposed to do, ask him to write down his passwords as he was struggling to breathe?"

Martin did not have a will, so attorneys arranged for Pam to become his personal representative, the administrator of his estate. But obtaining Martin's Apple password required a court order, the lawyers explained. "I never dreamed it could be so expensive just to obtain basic information," Pam said.

Apple was not her only problem. As she tried to access other financial accounts, she found she did not know the answers to his security questions, like "Who is your best friend?" She knew Martin's best friend, and yet, when she entered that name, it was not the right answer.

Her final comment to me was, "It's amazing when someone dies, all the work you have to do on top of grieving. It has been very overwhelming. I wish we had put our stuff in order and that we had prepared. Knowing what I know now, I would tell young people that they need wills and financial plans, too."

I could relate to what both Katie and Pam experienced. Like Katie, I did not have the energy to fight Bucky's partners, so I gave in, and as with Pam and Martin, Bucky and I did not share financial information. He paid all the household bills and, of course, those of his law firm. When he died, I was mired in financial problems that I knew little about.

To better understand how widows end up in such financial turmoil, I turned to two financial advisors, Craig Ratz and Grant Lindaman. Craig has been a Certified Financial Planner™ and consultant for twenty-five years, working to help individuals, families, and business owners achieve their financial goals. Grant began a career in financial planning in the 1970s. He co-founded New Era Financial Group in 1982 and New Era Financial Advisors in 1986. He currently serves as president of both firms.

I started my interviews with Craig and asked him how couples can prepare financially for the death of a spouse. He told me the salient question he asks every client is, "Who knows what you know?"

Craig said he sees cases where a husband dies and the wife does not know what he knew about finances and vital accounts. In those cases, problems can turn into nightmares.

Craig told me that everyone loves to talk about investments or refinancing their mortgages, the kind of stuff he refers to as the "societal sexy stuff." But he finds very few people want to talk about the issues that are impactful to their life if someone does not come home.

He encourages all of his clients, if their spouse is still alive, to start having tough conversations. He asks them to think about what the experience will be like if one of them dies. What are the things their spouse will need? He finds that when people give it some thought, they realize they will be leaving their spouse in the lurch if they don't put some key things down on paper.

In Craig's business, he most often deals with a surviving spouse who is a woman. Sometimes she is not necessarily the one who knew the financial information or who delved into that realm. He observed that is often a generational artifact, and he sees it less often with younger generations.

I told him that I had not been involved in our financial decisions and asked him why he thought so many women don't get involved. He said that, in part, that happens because in many relationships, each partner has specific roles. In many cases, he sees it was the husband who took care of the finances while the wife managed the other aspects of their lives. It's just as true that surviving spouses who are men might not know where to find their children's inoculation records or who the tradesmen are who handle their household maintenance.

Craig explained that a division of labor is fine, but couples need to share information. If they do not have a plan or have not shared what each of them knows, the surviving spouse ends up making life-altering mistakes.

ORGANIZE YOUR LIFE FOR DEATH

Craig told me that everyone should prepare a binder that contains all the things both spouses need to know, such as account numbers, contact numbers, addresses, passwords, and the like. Electronic files are fine, but he says to also consider having a print copy available. The information should be kept where it is easily accessible.

Craig encourages couples to become the chief financial officers of their household, so when a spouse dies, they are able to move on with their finances without skipping a beat.

Sometimes a binder of information can become critical while a spouse is still alive; for example, if they become mentally incapacitated.

Craig explained that age-related mental decline is an ever-increasing problem in our society, and many spouses find that they lose their partner mentally long before they lose them physically. He sees clients where a spouse's memory has begun to fail, and they forget to do important tasks. He had a case where the person responsible for paying the mortgage suffered from dementia and forgot to pay it for months. Unfortunately, their house ended up in foreclosure.

He says that if key financial information is not documented—if people do not have that binder or have not maintained records—something is going to get missed. When things fall through the cracks is when clients are most at risk of falling prey to unscrupulous people.

Craig admitted that in his industry, as well as accounting and law, there can be bad actors who may be relying on a client to trust them. Unfortunately, that misplaced trust means they may not have the client's best interests in mind. He told me, "You are always your own best advocate. If something doesn't feel right, ask questions or get a second opinion."

He stressed that is one of the main reasons it is important to have competent advisors in place while both spouses are alive. Then, if the surviving spouse is not interested in learning all the ins and outs of accounts and plans, the advisor knows the family and their situation. Whether it is an estate attorney, insurance advisor, or financial consultant, it is important that someone knows the complete picture. He emphasized that the best time to work on a relationship with an advisor is not during a time of stress or tragedy; those relationships need to be built well before they are needed.

In my conversation with Grant, he also confirmed that a client with dementia is a big problem for advisors. He said he can usually spot someone struggling with dementia before the family does. He can tell by the questions they ask or the repeating of questions. He also emphasized that good financial plans need to be in place before dementia takes hold.

I knew from experience that the key to preventing problems and organizing for death lies with establishing a relationship with a trusted financial advisor. But how does one go about finding such a person?

HOW TO SELECT A TRUSTED ADVISOR

When I asked Grant how to go about selecting a financial advisor, the first thing he said was, "Don't be afraid of gray hair." He said finding an experienced, trusted advisor is not easy, but experience is key. He related that when he was in his forties, everything was theoretical. He believes that most attorneys, investment counselors, and accountants would say the same thing. Now that he is in his sixties, it is no longer theoretical for him; he has a lot of practical experience. He has seen friends and friends' spouses die and witnessed the turmoil in their lives from the level of someone close to them, not through the clinical eye of a professional.

Grant said his firm tells their clients that the most crucial choice they make is deciding who will advise them. As Grant puts it, "Everyone needs to find the right quarterback." He defines that person as someone who is not just the right financial advisor, or right legal advisor, or right accountant, but is someone who will look over all the issues at once and help avoid minefields. He tells widowed people that they do not need to grasp the issues 100 percent, but they do need to have someone with whom they can have an open conversation about them.

Craig gave me similar advice. He said that without a plan in place, widowed people may turn to advisors with whom they have never previously worked.

If a client does not currently have good advisors, he advises them to ask their friends for referrals. Craig said they should specifically ask them to recommend an estate planning group and an accounting group that have experience in administering estates.

He said when interviewing an advisor, people should ask how many estates a year they settle. He suggested they ask to talk to someone the advisor is currently working with—and that is key. Craig says it is very important to try to connect with people who are five years down this road. They will have learned from their experience and can share what they did right and wrong. They can help formulate what questions to ask any advisor.

Grant brought up another subject where the right financial advisor can be essential: family disagreements. He told me that in his experience, family members commonly have disagreements after a death. In his business, they try to cover all the what-ifs in their planning with clients, but it is unrealistic to assume that every possibility can be planned for. He says that is why it is so important to have someone who can help navigate the ebbs and flows of settling an estate. Everyone needs an advisor who does not judge but simply walks alongside to ensure everything gets taken care of properly. He believes that is by far the most important piece.

As I learned more about what should be done to get financial affairs in order and selecting the right advisor, I couldn't help but think about my friend Nancy, who was introduced in Chapter One. She inherited life insurance money when her husband, Bill, died. But without the right advisor in place, she spent it unwisely and ended up in a financial mess.

Nancy and Bill were married for more than thirty years when he was diagnosed with prostate cancer. He underwent years of expensive treatment.

Before that devastating diagnosis, the couple had been providing financial support for the caretaking of two aging parents. As the bills piled up, they added a second and then a third mortgage to their home. Eventually, the cancer took Bill's life, and Nancy was left with crushing debt.

Nancy was the beneficiary of Bill's $300,000 life insurance policy. In her grief, rather than consulting with a trusted advisor, she did what she said all "good girls" were taught to do: She used the money to pay down her debts.

The funds allowed her to pay off the second and third mortgages, but, unfortunately, she still faced a mountain of medical bills and her ongoing living and caretaking expenses. In the end, the debt overwhelmed her. She lost her home in foreclosure.

HOW TO HANDLE LIFE INSURANCE MONEY

I asked Craig about how surviving spouses should handle life insurance money. Craig advised that Nancy, rather than paying off mortgages, would have been better off using half of the life insurance money to pay off some debt and keeping half in cash. He explained that there is good debt and bad debt. An example of bad debt is a large balance on a credit card that is charging a high interest rate. But a mortgage might be considered good debt because the interest rate is low and holding a mortgage could provide a tax benefit; it is the cheapest credit you can get.

Unfortunately, in Craig's practice, he sees life insurance money used incorrectly quite often because the surviving spouse does not understand that the purpose of life insurance money is to maintain cash flow.

In addition, he said that quite often, people do not know what to do when they get a sudden windfall of money. They do not have experience in managing substantial amounts of money, so they do not know what to do, how to do it, or how to work with the cash flow. He said, "Think of all the lottery winners who end up broke." The unfamiliarity with managing large sums of money is why it is critical to have a trusted advisor in place well beforehand.

Craig also stressed that it is important to have an idea of how, when, and where assets go in the event of a death or who has access to those assets in the case of incapacity. He has seen cases where the assets are tied up in estate settlement for close to two years, and the surviving spouse has limited or no access to those funds. He explained that settling an estate takes time, and sometimes the optimal result from an income tax or an estate planning point of view creates short-term issues. He asks clients how they would manage if that happened. He encourages them to make sure there is enough access to bank accounts and other assets for the survivor.

Shortly after my discussions with Craig and Grant, I had a long conversation with Andrew, a friend who is a financial advisor with a major brokerage company. He agreed with the advice that I had received thus far but added one unique suggestion: Write a letter of intention.

I was intrigued. I had never heard of an intention letter, so I asked him to explain more about them.

WHY YOU SHOULD CONSIDER INTENTION LETTERS

Andrew said most of his clients seek his advice because they want to position their assets to avoid unnecessary taxes and ensure an effective transition of assets to future generations. But some clients have a different goal—maintaining control of their assets after their death. He said that most often, these people are former business owners, executives, or other individuals accustomed to a high level of control in their lives. That tends to result in them being uncomfortable giving up control of assets or decision-making, even after death.

Andrew told me these clients create rules that will govern their estate and its disbursement after their death, which is a form of leading the family from beyond the grave. These rules could make the estates difficult to manage, especially if the deceased person provided no context for the family about his or her decisions and left no intention letter.

Andrew explained that intention letters are key to conveying a person's wishes—and the concept is exactly as it sounds. These letters are written to the family by the author to express his or her intentions for their money and estate plan and the values they hope will carry on past their death. In essence, it is writing down what they hope their legacy will be.

Andrew said that estate documents, including an intention letter, are critical for people of all ages to put in place. In his experience, he said the number one reason young couples do not create an estate plan is they do not know, or cannot agree, about who gets their children in case of their deaths. But leaving an intention letter for young children is key because whoever ends up raising the children will cherish guidance about what the parents would have wanted for them. It is also an opportunity to write down values for the children. Such a letter could give the children a sense of who their parent or parents were.

Andrew finds that the more complex the rules of an estate, the more important an intention letter becomes. He said a client may express their intentions to an attorney, but by the time the attorney drafts those thoughts into legal documents, the feeling and emotion that guided that intention—the key context—can get lost.

Andrew pointed out that intention letters provide a written documentation in the client's own words about his or her wishes. One of the most common problems Andrew encounters is when the rules applied to the distribution of a trust state that heirs must turn a certain age before receiving their share. This rule can be awkward, especially if it is applied to one child but not another.

Andrew said that without an intention letter in place, where the parent explains the reason for such a decision, the person facing the restriction can feel a tremendous amount of resentment toward the deceased or other siblings. An intention letter can explain why the decision was made, including past experiences. For example, if a child has a history of unwise financial decisions, the parent can explain that they hope to save the child from losing all their inheritance in a short period of time.

I learned from Andrew that intention letters are also useful in the distribution of assets, such as a family home or vacation property. Deceased parents may want to pass the property to the next generation, so it continues as a family gathering place. This is especially true with vacation homes and family cabins. But in his experience, Andrew said that rather than bringing the family together, it often causes a rift. Ideally, the letter should not only explain why the property was passed along but also stipulate what should happen if there is no agreement about keeping it.

He has observed situations where some family members may enjoy the family vacation home, while others do not. There are expenses associated with property that can create tension about who uses it and how often. He said arguments frequently arise about whether to keep the home or put it up for sale, and there is usually at least one sibling who says, "I know what Mom and Dad would have wanted," or "Mom and Dad would be appalled that you want to sell this house."

Andrew's clients who have an intention letter included in their estate plan leave no doubt about what they want to happen.

Another problem Andrew sees is when one parent in a blended family dies. He said all too often, the children of the deceased believe that a surviving stepparent is not adhering to what their parent would have wanted. Frequently, they do not understand why the parent left the entirety of an estate to the stepparent.

Again, this is where Andrew said an intention letter can be useful. It can contain language as simple as, "It is important to me that my wife is taken care of for her lifetime." That eliminates the argument that the distribution is not what the deceased person truly intended.

Andrew told me that another major issue for clients is how to treat their beneficiaries fairly. He observed that fair is not always equal, and equal is not always fair.

Andrew explained that the fair-and-equal problem most often arises in families where one child has been successful financially while another has not. The parent may provide more money in the estate for the child who has less money because, in their estimation, their more successful child does not need as much help. That can create tensions between the siblings. He has seen unequal distributions interpreted as "Mom and Dad loved you more." Unfortunately, he said it is not unusual to see siblings break apart and stop talking to one another after an unequal distribution.

If the parent has an intention letter in place, it can help provide a justification for the difference in distribution. Andrew said it might not make the beneficiary who feels slighted any happier, but at least they have context and can be assured that the decision was not based on favoritism.

Once Andrew explained the concept of intention letters, I knew that was something I needed to add to my estate plan. But I wasn't sure where to start, so I asked his advice on how to begin.

He told me some clients have great difficulty writing an intention letter; they don't want to think about their own demise or what will happen to their money. He finds that is why so many people procrastinate when it comes to putting estate documents in place. He said, "We fool ourselves into thinking that we are going to die in our sleep at age 104. But that is not realistic."

Andrew pointed out that when people are putting together a will or estate plan, they have already made the leap to considering what will happen after their death, which makes it an opportune time to write an intention letter. In fact, Andrew believes the intention letter can become the most important document a person completes. He said that is especially true for someone who is trying to control things from the grave or has placed lots of rules around distributions because it provides context for those decisions. It can prevent resentment and hard feelings.

Andrew said the secret to starting an intention letter is to just start writing. He said you can just put one thing down on paper and set it aside. Then go back to it when you are ready and write the next thing. It is a lot like exercise and eating more healthfully, other things we know we should do but tend to put off. In his experience, once people begin, the ball is rolling, and most end up completing it.

He noted that intention letters are unlike other estate planning documents in that they are not legally binding documents, but rather a personal expression of beliefs and wishes. No one else needs to read or prepare it. In fact, he said some clients seal the letter and ask that it be opened only after their death.

Andrew has observed that some clients choose to make their intention letters deeply emotional and personal. He often shares stories with his clients about how these letters have been helpful to other clients and how a lack of one has caused stress. He emphasizes with them that anytime you can remove stress following a death in the family, it helps eliminate other problems.

There were so many unknowns when Bucky died—by the time he became ill, he did not have the time or focus to discuss his wishes, much less commit them to paper. I realize now that this is something we both should have done.

I asked Andrew how he handles intention letters when both partners in a marriage seek his counsel. He said he often asks spouses to write intention letters separately and then meet with him to talk about what they've written. He said it is not unusual for them to read each other's letters and realize that they are not on the same page about their plans, which has sparked some good conversations. He said some clients say they wish they'd had the conversation twenty years prior because it would have changed their financial decisions. In these instances, Andrew said the intention letter provides context in real-time, versus after death.

He told me about a couple he worked with where the wife wrote her letter shortly after he suggested it, but the husband kept putting it off. With a bit of prodding, the husband finally wrote a little, and then put it aside. He gave it more thought and wrote some more. Eventually, he wrote twelve pages. He was able to put in writing what made him the man he was, what values he tried to instill in his family, and what he wanted his legacy to be. He edited the document numerous times—until it was something of which he was enormously proud. He told Andrew it was one of the greatest things he ever did.

When I left Andrew, I went home and did something that I should have done long ago: I wrote an intention letter to my two daughters.

LESSONS LEARNED ABOUT FINANCIAL PLANNING:

- Seek the counsel of a trusted financial advisor.
- If you don't have an advisor, get recommendations from people you trust.
- Place all of your important information in a binder, including lists of account numbers and passwords.
- After the death of a spouse, ensure that you understand your cash flow and how to best use life insurance proceeds.
- Include an intention letter in your estate documents.

CHAPTER FOUR:
DAD NEVER TOLD US THAT
The Quandary of Stepchildren

"LIFE AIN'T ALWAYS BEAUTIFUL,
SOMETIMES IT'S JUST PLAIN HARD.
LIFE CAN KNOCK YOU DOWN,
IT CAN BREAK YOUR HEART."
Gary Allan

STEPMOTHER: THE VERY word invokes a degree of angst. Growing up, we didn't read fairy tales about stepfathers, but stories were replete with evil stepmothers, from *Cinderella* to *Snow White*. While her husband is alive, a stepmother's relationship with her husband's children might seem close and loving, but my interviews revealed that after her husband's death, a stepmother's relationship with his children can become embattled and broken.

Frequently, the squabbles are about money, or as one expert said, "Loving step-relationships that have been in place for decades break up over $10,000."

I heard many stories from widows about family problems, but perhaps none were more heartbreaking than those that involved stepchildren.

As you've read in previous chapters, my friend Nancy encountered numerous problems after her husband died. The most poignant was the breakdown of her thirty-year relationship with her stepdaughter.

Nancy had a wonderful, loving relationship with Susie, Bill's daughter from his first marriage. Throughout Bill's illness and their care for aging parents, Susie had shown little interest in Bill and Nancy's financial affairs. Consequently, she was unaware of the staggering medical and caretaking bills that had piled up. She thought her dad had all the money in the world, so when Bill died, Susie assumed that she would get a sizable inheritance.

Nancy had the unenviable task of telling Susie that there was no inheritance because there was no money. Susie refused to believe it, even after Nancy outlined the medical and caretaking expenses plus the three mortgages against the house. She was furious with Nancy, whom she believed was withholding her rightful inheritance.

"That's *not* what my father would have wanted," Susie declared.

A thirty-year relationship with Susie that Nancy believed to be a loving one broke down over money.

Nancy said, "All Susie cared about was a handout. She would not believe me when I told her there was no money. I was so vulnerable. I had just lost Bill, and the last thing I wanted was to lose Susie, too. What I discovered is that sometimes a stepchild does not care about your struggle as much as they care about the money."

I learned from the estate attorneys and financial advisors I spoke with that it is common to see problems with blended families after the death of a parent. One day, while I was playing golf, I mentioned this issue to my partner and she told me about her friend, Linda. Linda did everything possible to avoid problems with her stepchildren when she settled her husband's estate. She was terrified of losing the relationship with them and not being able to see her step-grandchildren. Yet, despite her best intentions, the family connections ruptured once her husband died. I wanted to know more about why her plans went awry, so I arranged to speak with Linda by phone to learn more about her experience.

Linda told me she and her husband, Stuart, had been married twenty-eight years when he died. He suffered a heart attack and then was diagnosed with Hodgkin's lymphoma. He sought treatment, but eventually, the doctors informed Stuart that they had exhausted all the options.

In addition to Linda, Stuart also left behind three middle-aged children from his first marriage. Linda's relationship with her step-children had been a bit rocky for years. But to her surprise, they showered her with love during the more than two years of Stuart's illness, thanking her for all that she was doing for their dad. She described their relationship as close.

Stuart bequeathed his entire estate to Linda so that she would have sufficient funds during her lifetime. Stuart's children had never asked about an inheritance and were unaware that they would not inherit anything upon their father's death. Linda did not anticipate a problem over that issue; two of Stuart's children had more money than she and Stuart did. The third child had sometimes struggled more financially than the others but had also received more financial help from Stuart over the years.

When I first spoke with Linda shortly after Stuart's death, she told me that she planned to call each of the children before meeting with the attorney. She wanted to let them know that she was the sole beneficiary before the reading of the will. But in her grief, she did not have the energy to make those calls. Instead, she decided to let the attorney deliver the news.

Two weeks later, Linda called me. This time, she was sobbing. She told me that when the family gathered in the attorney's office, the children were angry when they heard Stuart's final wishes were to leave everything to Linda, and upon her death, any remaining money would go to his grandchildren.

The children's hurt was exacerbated by the legal tone used in the will: "For the purposes of this will, it will be as if Stuart's children have predeceased Stuart." In theory, Stuart killed off his children.

The children were hurt and angry—and immediately blamed Linda for not advising Stuart to name them as the successor beneficiaries, those who would receive the estate upon Linda's death. They felt she had a "golden opportunity," as they said, to advise Stuart that what he was doing was wrong. But Stuart believed that he had given his children significant monetary gifts throughout their lives—vacations, down payments for homes, and loans—and he was quite comfortable that any money remaining after Linda's death should go to his grandchildren.

In truth, Linda *had* urged Stuart to have a conversation with his children about his wishes, but he never did. Linda explained, "By that time, he was fighting for his life, and he was focused on his health, not, 'Oh my God, I'd better tell my kids I'm not leaving them any money.'"

To compound the problem, Stuart's children believed that his estate was worth much more than it was. Much of Stuart's retirement money had evaporated when he made a bad investment in a building in Chicago. It was a sizable loss, and consequently, his trust was never funded. Linda and Stuart had been living month-to-month on income from investments.

Once the three children understood that there was a diminished amount of money to claim, they took action to protect their children's share. They sent Linda a letter requesting that she set money aside to establish trusts for the grandchildren, funded with a meaningful amount. They stipulated that Linda could never access the money set aside for the grandchildren for any reason. Linda was taken aback. "They told me that would be a step in the right direction," she said.

Linda's financial advisor called Stuart's son to corroborate that Stuart did not have as much money as his children had assumed. The advisor also said he would never recommend to a woman in her sixties that she set aside money that she could never touch. He explained that Linda could live another twenty years, and it was impossible to determine with accuracy what her future financial needs might be. He emphasized that Stuart's wish was that Linda have her needs met during her lifetime.

The fallout from Stuart's beneficiary decision was immediate. Linda's relationship with her stepchildren broke down, and there was no communication with them for a period of time. Both Linda's therapist and financial advisor suggested that she keep her distance until emotions settled. Recently, they have taken steps to reconnect, and Linda is looking forward to the day when the relationships are completely healed.

I felt sorry for Linda, who had to deal with so many losses in such a short period of time. As I was interviewing widows and experts, problems with stepchildren cropped up in many of my conversations. I reached out to Susan Link, the estate attorney we heard from in Chapter Two, and Lynn Kiely, the psychotherapist in Chapter One, to weigh in on the problems that plague widows around the touchy subject of stepchildren and money.

THE NEED TO HAVE DIFFICULT CONVERSATIONS

Susan told me that Linda's situation is not unusual. It is common in settling estates to encounter problems with money and stepchildren. What she often hears is, "Dad never told me. I was very close to Dad, and he would have told me if this is what he wanted."

Her advice to clients who have blended families is that while the couple does not need to tell the kids the amount of their net worth, the birth parent *does* need to tell the kids that he or she is the one making decisions about the trusts and how the estate will be disbursed. She said that is vitally important. If that conversation does not take place, the stepchildren of the surviving spouse may believe the stepparent influenced those decisions and imposed his or her will.

I learned from Susan that many children never hear of the estate plan from their parents. She said most often that is because the parents may want to avoid any conflict over how the money will be disbursed. But Susan urges parents to communicate the allocation of their estate ahead of time in order to avoid a lot of misunderstanding and anger.

She acknowledged that these are hard conversations, but parents need to have them. And, if the children ask, "But why is she getting all this money when she isn't even our mother?" the parent needs to address it honestly. Answering these types of questions beforehand actually helps the children move on. If they do not hear it from the parent, they may continue to believe that it really was not what was supposed to happen.

Katie, my friend introduced in Chapter Three, learned the hard way that financial problems can bleed into family problems. As her husband, Chip, faced his terminal diagnosis, he asked his attorney and financial advisor to come to the house so he could make his final will. Wisely, he also asked his brother and sister to witness the process. Chip wanted some assurance for his four children that trusted family members had witnessed his final wishes. Katie felt comfortable with everything; he set up two trusts that would honor his children and honor what he wanted for her.

After Chip died, his children were surprised to learn of the humble size of Chip's estate. They were also furious when they learned that there were two trusts. Chip's children viewed Katie as the interceder and refused to believe that the arrangement was what their father wanted, despite the assurances of those who witnessed his signing of the final will.

Katie said that Chip's children were upset that he never told them how his estate would be divided. "Their opinion was that I didn't deserve anything. There were so many acrimonious meetings that I finally dissolved the trust and said, 'You take it, even though this is not what your dad wanted.' I just couldn't deal with it." The severed relationship was heartbreaking to Katie.

Looking back, Katie wishes she had insisted Chip talk to his kids in person about his wishes. At the time, she did not feel it was her place to tell him to include his children in that final meeting. It was his money and his decision. She now realizes that he did not want to face his children; he did not want any conflict as he was dying.

Katie and Chip faced an ugly truth: If things are not in order before you get sick, it is hard to get them in order *after* you are sick.

I sought advice from Lynn Kiely about how these family divisions can be avoided. In her psychotherapy practice, she sees blended families that have difficulty moving on after the death of the spouse or parent.

THE STEPPARENT GETS THE BLAME

Lynn told me that sometimes a newly widowed woman may feel blame from the children of her deceased spouse: blamed for his death, for the circumstances around his death, or for the distribution of assets. She said stepchildren may see their stepmother as the evil one who somehow conned their father into her plan. If relations with his children were ambivalent or shaky prior to his death, they may become more so afterward. Lynn sees that happen in many families, and sometimes relationships are destroyed because of it. That is why Lynn counsels that it is essential that people plan for their death—and that they talk to their families about it.

She often sees the tensions around "blood versus step" emerge after death, and views that as incredibly sad and unfortunate. She acknowledges that there is no easy solution. She tells her clients that the only thing they can do to repair damaged relationships is encourage those involved to express their feelings.

I told Lynn about the widows I spoke with and how money became the breaking point for these families. She advised that if a family is breaking apart over money, they should not just accept the split. They should do what they can do with the energy they have. She said that if a conversation would be too fraught with one or more of the children, perhaps write a letter or talk to those with whom there is still a connection.

But in the end, she said if nothing helps, eventually stepparents may have to just let go for their own mental health. She has observed that sometimes in their grief, the children need to be angry at somebody, and the stepparent is the easiest target. She acknowledges that is unfortunate and sad, but it is the reality. She summed it up this way: There are so many losses that reverberate from the loss of life that, sadly, sometimes the stepchild relationship is one of them.

After hearing so many sad stories about family discord, I was grateful I did not experience that pain. I can only imagine the difficulty of adding the loss of decades-long, loving stepchild relationships to the grief that already exists when a spouse dies.

LESSONS LEARNED ABOUT DEALING WITH STEPCHILDREN:

- The birth parent needs to have a conversation with his/her children about how their estate is structured and what they can expect upon the parent's death.

- If problems arise after the death of a spouse, a stepparent needs to keep the lines of communication open and be transparent about the estate documents and the thinking behind the distribution decisions.

- If all attempts at communication fail and the relationship with stepchildren remains toxic, the best course of action may be for the stepparent to step away from it for their own mental health.

CHAPTER FIVE:
SAYING THE LONG GOODBYE
The Ravages of Dementia

"BUT IT'S JUST YOU AND ME,
GOING THROUGH THE MILL,
CLIMBING UP A HILL,
THIS IS THE LONG GOODBYE."
Brooks and Dunn

I HAVE A CLOSE friend whose husband has Alzheimer's disease. He was a dashingly handsome and brilliant man, but over time the ravages of Alzheimer's slowly eroded his personality and mental alertness. Bucky and I always enjoyed spending time with this couple, so we continued to do so even as the symptoms of the husband's disease progressed. After an evening out with them, Bucky and I would talk about how difficult life must be for her. How could she maintain social relationships when her husband does not even know where he is or whom he is with?

I felt so sorry for both of them—and then Bucky died. Her husband is still alive, but he has no idea who she is. I have lain awake at night wondering which one of us is now leading the more difficult life.

I learned through this friend, and other friends similarly affected by a dementia diagnosis of their spouse, that it brings with it life-altering challenges that include emotional devastation, financial and legal custodianship, caregiving, and, worst of all, a loss of hope. Their stresses usually start well before their spouse's deaths; they lose companionship, a social life, and emotional support while their spouse is still alive.

One such widow was my friend, Kathryn. Kathryn and her husband, Jim, were set up on a blind date by their respective sisters. They were the perfect match in the estimation of all who knew them. Jim was living the whirlwind life of a US congressman when they started dating. Kathryn recalls that on their first date, he asked her what district she lived in—not the name of her representative, but the number of the district. Kathryn's career had been in business, not politics, so she knew the name but not the number.

Kathryn became Jim's steady companion at glittering Washington gatherings. She embraced the lifestyle and obligations with grace and enthusiasm. One of their first outings was to the White House Christmas party. Kathryn was impressed that both Republicans and Democrats made a point of telling her what a great guy Jim was.

Eventually, they married and established a life in both Minnesota and Washington, filled with politics, travel, social commitments, friends, and family. But as politics turned more partisan, Jim decided not to seek re-election. He wanted to retire while he was still young and healthy, and they were both excited to see what the next chapter of their lives would bring. They moved to Massachusetts, where Jim accepted a fellowship at Harvard, served on boards and did some consulting work. Life was not as busy, but it was good.

Over time, Kathryn noticed minor changes in Jim. He was a tall man, but his shoulders began to stoop and his driving became erratic. The changes were enough to alarm Kathryn, who confided in a friend who was a doctor. The doctor suggested Jim might have Parkinson's disease and should undergo testing to rule that out.

Jim did not have tremors, but the testing showed that he had memory issues. He could not draw a clock or repeat the five words the doctor had given him just a few minutes previously. The diagnosis finally came back as Lewy body disease, which Kathryn describes as an umbrella term for two related clinical diagnoses: "dementia with Lewy bodies" and "Parkinson's disease dementia." These disorders share the same underlying changes in the brain and very similar symptoms, but the symptoms appear in a different order, depending on where the Lewy bodies first form.

Kathryn knew there was no cure available, but she researched the disease to gather as much information as she could. She learned that while Lewy body is a form of dementia, it is different from Alzheimer's; there is not a gradual decline that keeps declining. For Jim, there were days when he was perfectly cognizant, where he and Kathryn enjoyed discussions about the world and politics as they always had. He continued to have good days—but he also had horrible days.

Then at about the three-year mark, Jim's illness took a turn for the worse. He began to experience typical Lewy body symptoms—hallucinations and delusions. Kathryn assured him they were not real, but Jim would not believe her. He was afraid and angry. He began calling the police. He was frustrated and did not understand where he was or what was going on around him. The following morning, he would have no recollection of the incident. Kathryn ultimately ended up hiring an additional person to help keep them and their caregivers safe.

Jim's body grew frailer. Kathryn could not let him sleep upstairs because he got up multiple times in the night, and she was afraid he would fall down the stairs.

Their world began to shrink. When Jim was in Congress, he had many friends, but with the progression of his disease, their social life dwindled down to three couples who were willing to go out with them. It was difficult to get Jim dressed and into the car to go out, so they would often have dinner at their home.

During Jim's illness, many people wanted to give Kathryn suggestions on how to move forward, but she chose to surround herself with a small group of friends and family to lean on for support and advice. She felt that reducing her world to just a few people was critical to her well-being.

Kathryn realized that Jim's decline had reached a pivotal point when a friend remarked, "Jim is actively dying. You need to bring in hospice care." Kathryn had been so immersed in the day-to-day existence of caring for Jim that she had not seen how much he had declined. Nor did she recognize how exhausted and in need of respite she was.

Jim was reluctant to talk with Kathryn about his disease, nor did he spend time researching Lewy body. He knew his disease was fatal because he felt it. Sometimes he shared with her the hurt that he physically felt—the rigidity and stiffness—and, occasionally, he acknowledged that his mind was not working as it normally had. But Jim chose to live life to the fullest on the days when he was feeling well, rather than dwelling on the effect the disease was taking on his mind and body.

Shortly before Jim died, one of Kathryn's friends urged her to get Jim's passwords and access to his online accounts. Although she felt it was an invasion of privacy, she now says it was one of the most important things she did, as it avoided problems after his death. Kathryn was fortunate that other aspects of dealing with Jim's death were already in place. Jim had his final wishes spelled out in what he called his "funeral file." After the attacks on the Capital on September 11, 2001, all members of Congress were asked to create a file that contained everything from Bible passages and hymns they wished to be included in their funeral service to who would deliver the eulogies. Each year, Jim reviewed the file with Kathryn and also scheduled a visit with their attorney to review all of his final wishes. After Jim's death, Kathryn was grateful that, as his trustee, she fully understood his wishes and could execute them exactly as he had wanted. Jim and Kathryn fought his Lewy body disease with courage and dignity, but Jim succumbed to it in the late fall of 2020, amid the COVID-19 pandemic. His funeral was limited to members of his immediate family, but tributes flowed in from people all over the country. Jim's peers lauded him as one of the last bipartisan, pragmatic politicians who was adept at problem-solving.

Today, Kathryn still struggles with shaping a new life without Jim. She is fortunate to have great family and friends that have supported her. She knows that eventually her life will evolve, and a new kind of life will emerge. In the meantime, she is comforted by the many friends of Jim who have surrounded her, and she is once again reaching out to her old friends to re-establish a social life. Still, as she says, "How do you replace your 50/50 partner?"

After speaking with Kathryn about Jim's experience with Lewy body, I decided to do more research about dementia, including Alzheimer's, which is the most common form of the disease. According to the Alzheimer's Association, the number of Americans living with Alzheimer's is growing—and growing fast. An estimated 6.5 million Americans aged 65 and older are living with Alzheimer's in 2022.

I reached out to Ronald C. Petersen, MD, PhD, to get his views on the disease, how it is diagnosed, and how patients, their families, and caregivers can best manage it. Dr. Petersen directs the Mayo Clinic Alzheimer's Disease Research Center and the Mayo Clinic Study of Aging. He has spent his career exploring cognitive changes in normal aging, mild cognitive impairment, and dementia.

WITH DEMENTIA, EARLY DETECTION IS KEY

Dr. Petersen confirmed what I had read: Cognitive dysfunctions, including mild cognitive impairment and dementia, are the leading causes of disease in aging. I told him my recollection is that years ago, when people lost some cognitive function, it was described as "hardening of the arteries" or "senility." I thought those types of mental decline were a normal part of aging. But Dr. Petersen told me that as a society, we are more aware of these cognitive changes in aging and now know that those changes are not necessarily normal.

I learned from him that some cognitive changes *are* normal and are experiences with which we can all relate. For example, you might not be able to remember the name of a person you used to work with. You might run into him in a grocery store and try to cover it by saying, "Hey, buddy, how are you doing?" Then fifteen minutes later, you remember that his name was Bill, and you chide yourself for forgetting that. But Dr. Petersen said that type of forgetfulness is quite common and is due to our loss of ability to multitask as we age.

What may not be normal aging is when you repeatedly start to forget important information that you formerly would have easily remembered, or those around you start to notice a decline. Dr. Petersen made the distinction that those types of changes may warrant further attention because some forms of dementia are due to other medical problems that have gotten out of control—side effects from medications, for example. He emphasized that any decline deserves a look by your primary physician.

Dr. Peterson told me that, realistically, if you are in your seventies or eighties and becoming progressively more forgetful to a significant degree, you need to be concerned about a degenerative disease of the brain. Of those diseases, Alzheimer's is the most common. One of the reasons we are seeing more dementia diagnoses is that people are living longer, so they are at greater risk for developing it.

Fortunately, he told me that physicians and their patients are more aware of cognitive diseases than in years past. It is common for a person in their sixties to be referred to him because they are becoming a bit more forgetful. Sometimes one of their parents had dementia and they worry that they are headed down the same road. Regardless of the motivation, he said because people are more attuned to the symptoms of dementia, they do not attribute cognitive changes to simply getting older.

Dr. Petersen explained that the medical community has improved its diagnostic skills and is now good at determining if someone is experiencing normal aging or if it goes beyond normal aging. If it is beyond normal aging, they can do imaging studies, PET scans or MRIs, that look inside the brain to see whether the amyloid proteins associated with Alzheimer's disease are present.

Dr. Petersen said the question people often ask after they receive a dementia diagnosis is, "What can be done about it?" and he said this is where the medical field has come up a bit short. There are some medications that may temporarily improve or slow the progression of symptoms. These treatments can sometimes help people with Alzheimer's disease maximize function and maintain independence for a time. But the fact remains that there is no treatment that cures Alzheimer's disease or alters the disease process in the brain. He told me some recent drug developments have been controversial, but he views them as an advancement in the field.

THE STIGMA OF DEMENTIA

Dr. Petersen reflected that when the tests indicate dementia, neither giving nor receiving that diagnosis is pleasant. He strives to be honest with the family and the patient because the reality is it is a fatal disease—not tomorrow or next week, or even two years from now, but eventually, the disease will kill. He says they can keep people functioning at a reasonably elevated level for as long as possible, but the fact remains that it is a progressive, degenerative disease. For that reason, he believes that dementia is a group diagnosis because it has implications for the entire family. Those implications can reach quite far into the future.

I mentioned to Dr. Petersen that I perceive people are ashamed to share a diagnosis of dementia. He agreed, saying he has seen this stigma firsthand when patients have been treated differently once others know they have dementia. He said it is unfortunate when that occurs because it is a brain disease, and it is just like having a disease of another organ. But because the brain is so important, because it controls our behavior, people have a different reaction to a dementia diagnosis.

He observed that society tends to relegate someone with a diagnosis of dementia to a less-than status. There is an assumption that the person does not understand things, or does not comprehend, or cannot participate in decision-making, and that may not be the case.

Dr. Petersen explained that in various stages and types of dementia, conditions can fluctuate, so there may be times when the person is perfectly lucid, able to make decisions and participate in activities with the family. A day later, or two days later, he or she may be really confused about where they are or who their spouse is. That fluctuation in behavior does result in a stigma more often than not.

He believes that society is getting better at eliminating that stigma, but the change is coming very slowly. Dr. Petersen has conversations with patients and their spouses about whether or not to tell their children about the diagnosis. Some people also worry that the neighbors will find out about their diagnosis. Ultimately, he said there is no right or wrong answer about whom a patient chooses to tell; that decision is personal. He does recommend that people share the diagnosis with close family members because that provides an opportunity to educate them on what it means, which can reduce the stigma.

Dr. Petersen cited the most salient example of keeping a diagnosis private was the case with Ronald and Nancy Reagan. She did not want Alzheimer's disease to be his signature. She did not want people to think of him as the president who died of Alzheimer's. He had a whole life that preceded his illness, a life where he was highly active and served the public. She kept him out of the limelight and restricted his visits because she did not want people to associate him with the disease, though she allowed some research institutes to use their names in some ways.

Dr. Petersen said other families have gone in the opposite direction. A few years ago, Mayo Clinic did a documentary film called *I'll Be Me*, about Glen Campbell in his later years after his Alzheimer's diagnosis. He went on tour after his diagnosis and talked freely about his disease.

Although some people choose to keep their diagnosis private, I told Dr. Petersen that I've observed many more friends and acquaintances speaking out about receiving a dementia diagnosis. In part, Dr. Petersen said that is because more people are being diagnosed with Mild Cognitive Impairment (MCI), which is an intermediate form of dementia. This means that instead of going from normal aging to dementia, the early diagnosis of MCI allows the patient and his doctor to address the issues they currently face and those that may come in the future.

He said that typically, a person with MCI does not remember things as well as they used to, or as well as they ought to, but everything else is intact. They may not be as efficient as they used to be, but they are still driving a car, paying household bills, and doing the taxes. To the casual observer, the person seems more normal than not. But physicians may notice that things are not what they ought to be, and that is when they diagnose MCI.

GOOD PLANNING IS KEY
TO MANAGING LIFE WITH MCI

Dr. Petersen said that when doctors diagnose a patient with MCI, they also discuss the need to plan for the future. He stresses that they may be perfectly fine for another five to eight years, but there is no way of knowing the rate at which the disease is going to progress. It could progress rapidly, so he encourages patients and their families to put plans in place quickly. He believes it is important to plan for the worst and hope for the best.

Because of the uncertainty about how MCI will progress, he tries to be delicate in how he describes the disease to the patient. He normally tells patients they can still participate in decisions or household management, but it is important to have someone else sit with them. Normally that person is the spouse, but whoever that person is, they need to work together to go over the bills, write checks, review taxes, and perform other important financial tasks. He believes that the sooner one can intervene in those kinds of shared activities, the better off the family will be.

He emphasized that another reason it is important to have these interventions early is that if they wait until their disease is at the dementia stage, it becomes tricky because, by definition, people have lost some capacity to engage in these activities. He acknowledged that most people are very reluctant to give up their responsibilities or share what had previously been their domain.

My conversation with Dr. Petersen about preparing for the worst reminded me of a discussion I had with Maggie Green, the estate attorney introduced in Chapter Two. She told me that she sees problems with dementia clients all the time. Ideally, her clients have a plan in place to transfer responsibility for financial issues and health care when one spouse becomes incapacitated. But even when there is a plan, there are often problems because the person with dementia does not want to sign over control of everything to their designated person or persons.

Maggie advised that the best way to avoid problems with transferring power is to have established trigger points that the spouses agree to before any mental decline starts. Some people designate a trusted physician to be the decision-maker, or alternatively, they select a committee of three family members or friends to perform that role. Still others require that both a doctor and the committee members need to agree that the client is incapacitated.

Dr. Petersen and Maggie both stressed that everyone, regardless of their age, should establish contingencies in the event they become incapable of making good decisions. Although mental incapacity most often happens as we age, younger people can also be affected. The key to avoiding problems is for the person with dementia to sign off on contingency plans while they are still of sound mind and body. That eliminates any argument after the fact about who should be making decisions, and that alone can prevent unnecessary family squabbles and legal expenses.

I know some of my friends have struggled with taking responsibilities away from their spouses. Dr. Petersen said he recognizes that it can be very stressful for family members to tell their loved ones that a part of their life has to end. Consequently, he tries to take the burden off the family by being the "bad guy" who delivers news the patient does not want to hear about limiting their activities and responsibilities. He said it is especially true when it comes to driving, particularly with men. Oftentimes he has the conversation with the patient, acknowledging that, for instance, taking away the car keys is a threat to their independence and that he hates to do it, but it has become necessary. He feels it is better that he be the bad guy rather than the wife or husband.

As my conversation with Dr. Petersen continued, I couldn't help but think about my friends who had been caregivers to their husbands during their journey through dementia. My three months of caring for Bucky had been exhausting, both mentally and physically. I can't imagine the toll it takes to provide care for a dementia patient, potentially for years.

When I asked Dr. Petersen about caregiving, he told me it can be a real problem because dementia can be a very protracted illness, especially if the person is in good general health. He noted that it is not an abrupt cardiac issue or a rapidly progressing cancer, it is a slow neurological degenerative disease of the brain.

CAREGIVERS, TAKE CARE OF YOURSELVES TOO

Dr. Petersen said that families handle things in different ways but cited studies that indicate caring for someone with dementia is extremely hard on caregivers, both medically and personally. Additionally, he said the primary caregiver may even be subjected to a higher incidence of cognitive impairment. He emphasized that he stops short of saying caregiving leads to dementia and would not want people to infer from his comment that caregivers are predisposed to developing dementia themselves; he thinks there might just be a statistical association. But he said there is no doubt that caring for a person with dementia is stressful and can bring out some subtle cognitive difficulties.

I told Dr. Petersen I believe that my friends whose husbands have dementia actually lose their husbands twice. He corroborated that is a sad fact about the disease. He said when a person is married to someone with dementia, they lose their life partner, and that takes away from what they can be or what they can do. How they deal with that depends on their support system, but he acknowledged that it really is a major loss to a couple when one of them develops dementia.

For that reason, the doctor insists that the spouses of his patients take care of themselves. He said the inclination of some people is to dive right into the caretaker tasks, saying, "We've been together for fifty years, we're dedicated to each other, and I won't let him/her go through this alone."

He said that is an appropriate response, but they need to realize that they also must take care of themselves. He stresses to all caregivers that they will be a better partner or caregiver if they also think about their own well-being. If they insist on being with their spouse 24/7, he tells them that will be hard, and they may not be performing at their best for their partner at that point. I learned from him that despite good intentions, all caregivers need breaks. They need to get away so they can get refreshed and recharge their batteries.

I asked Dr. Petersen what should happen when a caregiver just can't provide the level of care required by the dementia patient. He said it is exceedingly difficult for a caregiver to make the decision about whether to place their partner in a care facility. Not only is it difficult, but it can also be heartbreaking for many people. However, he said when it gets to the point that the patient requires day-to-day care, like bathing, or if the person is incontinent, it really degrades the relationship to a certain extent.

He advises that if the patient is at the stage of the disease where he or she needs that kind of care, it may be better to place them in a facility and let the staff take care of the twenty-four-hour personal needs. Then when the spouse comes to visit, they are a social partner; they may help in feeding but are not there for health and hygiene maintenance. The quality of the interaction between patient and spouse will be much better. They might even be able to go on walks together or go for a car ride outside the care facility.

The most significant question Dr. Petersen asks caregivers is, "If your spouse could participate in the decision, would he want you to be taking care of all his needs?" He said that, almost always, they say "no."

He went on to say that when the caregiver thinks about it that way, it can reduce some of the guilt they endure when having to place their spouse in a facility. The caregiver gets a sense of relief, knowing that the spouse would agree with that decision if they were still capable of making decisions. It allows them to move on in a better frame of mind.

As I listened to Dr. Petersen speak about caregiving and the toll it takes, I thought about my friend, Adele, a friend I have played golf with for the past thirty years. You learn a lot about a person on the golf course. In fact, my dad used to tell me you learn *everything* you need to know about a person on the golf course. I have found that to be true.

Walking down the fairways all those years, I learned a lot about Adele and her family. Adele took care of her mother, who developed dementia but lived a very long life. After her mother died, Adele's husband began to exhibit symptoms of the same illness. Once again, she was the caretaker.

None of this has been easy for Adele, but I never heard her complain or feel sorry for herself. She is remarkable in so many ways and was gracious in sharing her story.

Adele and her husband, Bill, were married for sixty-one years. She is not certain when Bill developed Alzheimer's disease, but it was their dog, Charles, who provided the first clue that something was amiss.

Bill doted on Charles and did everything for him—buying his dog food, taking him to the vet, making sure he got groomed, and, of course, giving him a daily walk. So, it was apparent something was wrong when one day Bill did not feed the dog or take him out for his walk. He never said he could not do those tasks; he just stopped doing them. Adele quietly assumed care for Charles, and they never spoke about their reversal of roles.

Soon, Bill stopped paying the bills. Again, Adele took over their financial affairs. They were avid duplicate bridge players, but Adele noticed that Bill's bridge skills were declining, and he would often make remarks that were non sequiturs. Bill began to ask Adele to walk in front of him when they were out; she now believes it was because he did not know where he was going. These were all signs, she says, but in the beginning, they were not too bad, so she continued to cover up for him.

Adele never had a discussion with Bill about his mental confusion. "The worst thing you can do is argue," Adele says. "If it was a sunny day but Bill said it was raining, I would just agree with him. I didn't want to cause him any more anxiety."

Adele finally convinced Bill to have a physical. The doctor ordered a battery of tests, and Bill was subsequently diagnosed with dementia, most likely Alzheimer's. Among other things, he told Adele that Bill should no longer drive a car.

She dreaded taking Bill's driving privileges away. Bill had spent his career in the car business, so cars were a big part of his identity.

She had heard horrible stories about wives wrenching the car keys away from their husbands, who would then turn violent. With some trepidation, Adele sat Bill down and explained that he should no longer drive the car and how the extra money from the sale of his car might come in handy. To her surprise, he went to the dealership with her, handed over the title to the car, and walked away. He never spoke of the car again.

Adele did not have close relatives nearby, so she joined an Alzheimer's support group to talk about Bill's disease and what she was experiencing. "Reading a book is not the same as listening to people who have experienced what you are going through," she said. "Until you've lived it, you have no idea how Alzheimer's will affect you." Adele became a huge advocate of peer support groups. She got practical advice from the women in her group about everyday challenges, such as changing the locks in the house or hiding the keys if Bill started to wander off.

The group also helped Adele realize that she was no longer dealing with Bill as a person; she was dealing with Alzheimer's, the disease. She was careful about where they went and what they did so as not to overly confuse or agitate Bill. Even going to the movies required that she find seats where they could make a quick exit if necessary.

She learned that, as frustrated as she got at times, she should not get mad at Bill because the Bill she knew and loved really was not there anymore. She began to lose "her Bill" little by little. She accepted that because there is no cure, the disease would eventually take over completely.

Good friends did not come to see Bill, and some never even called. Adele knows that she could have reached out to them, but caretaking kept her busy, and she did not think they would understand what she and Bill were going through.

When caring for Bill at home became too difficult, she placed him in a memory care facility. She visited him every day, ensuring that he had everything he needed and was being cared for properly. Then the COVID-19 pandemic hit. The care facility limited Adele's visits to three times per week for thirty minutes. Bill was confused about why Adele was not coming. The home would not even allow her to come to Bill's window. Explaining anything to Bill was difficult, but explaining COVID-19 was impossible. Adele was lonely and stressed, and to compound her problems, she was isolated due to the pandemic.

In addition to her other problems, Adele had to fight with their long-term care insurance carrier. Twenty years prior, a good friend had talked them into purchasing the policy. Adele assumed that would make her life easier once Bill entered the facility, but that was not the case. The company took months to reimburse Adele for Bill's care. Each month she dutifully submitted the invoices and claim, and each month they said it needed review. His diagnosis and prognosis did not change, but still, they insisted on a new review every month. In the interim, Adele was drawing down her savings account to pay the bills.

Then one morning, two people from the memory care facility came to the house. They told her that Bill had been rushed to the hospital and offered to take her there to see him. They were in the waiting room for five minutes when a doctor came to tell her that Bill had died from cardiac arrest.

Adele was distraught that after sixty-one years of marriage, Bill died alone. When the hospital allowed her into Bill's room, he was lying on a table, hooked up to tubes. This was not the last memory she wanted of her beloved husband.

Adele believes that Bill died because of COVID-19. Not because of the virus, but because of the federal guidelines placed on health care providers that resulted in Bill not receiving attention and routine visits from her. Day after day, Bill sat alone in his room, with minimal human interaction. She believes that if the care facility had allowed her to keep her normal visit routine, he might still be alive.

Adele is now alone and feeling a bit vulnerable. She has no children or relatives nearby, so there is no one to talk to or to help her out. She has experienced problems with car repairs and roof leaks, convinced that she is being taken advantage of because she is older. "I'm eighty," she says, "but I don't tell anyone my age because young people think eighty is dead."

Adele repeats the Serenity Prayer and cries almost every day. She is determined to "just deal with it" and stay strong because she has no other option. Each day, she thanks God that she is alive and healthy. She is thinking of moving to a retirement home so she will be cared for when and if her health begins to fail.

Adele's good attitude prevails through all her tribulations. She told me, "I really don't know what I'm going to do in the future. For now, I'm going to smile and continue on with life."

Adele's story was heartbreaking to hear and led me to do more research about dementia and the effect it has on caregivers. I sought an expert who could provide advice on how to best navigate the world of dementia care and support. I found Tami Kolbinger, care navigator and educator for the Central Minnesota Dementia Community Action Network. The mission of the network is to improve the access and quality of dementia care in their community. I spoke with Tami by phone to get her insight on how to best manage life before—and after—such a devastating diagnosis.

Tami talked a bit about how she became an expert in dementia care. She had been a successful marketing professional, juggling a career with marriage and two small children, when her mother suffered a heart attack and died. After she began to look after her widowed father, Tami realized that he was acting out of character. The doctors eventually diagnosed him with Alzheimer's disease. Tami became her father's full-time caregiver, easing up on her marketing career as she learned the ropes of assisting someone with dementia and caring for her dad.

Through her struggles, Tami saw a need for better education and resources—for both patients and caregivers. She wanted to improve dementia care, so she returned to school to become a certified dementia practitioner. Her experiences led her to focus on education for healthcare professionals, support for families and caregivers, and improving the lives of those living with dementia.

THE IMPORTANCE OF A SPECIFIC DIAGNOSIS

In my discussion with Tami, I learned that there are more than 120 types of dementia, each of them unique. She said people often interchange the word "dementia" with Alzheimer's, which she believes is a mistake. Dementia is most often caused by Alzheimer's disease, but many other diseases cause their own forms of dementia. Parkinson's disease is different from Lewy body disease, which is different from frontotemporal dementia, vascular dementia, or Alzheimer's disease.

Tami emphasized that how you care for people with these dementia diseases varies. Her father had Alzheimer's, and her father-in-law is currently battling Parkinson's, and her approach to care for each is different. She noted that Alzheimer's hallmark symptom is memory loss, but with Parkinson's, the person's memory can be completely intact. So, for instance, they educate her father-in-law's caregivers by letting them know that while he cannot speak, his mind is still good, and he is aware of everything going on around him.

In her experience, she has seen a lot of inconsistency in how dementia is defined and a lot of misinformation about the diseases that cause it. She said many times, primary care doctors diagnose people with dementia and tell patients to return in six months for a progress check, with no referrals to experts or additional support.

She said, "Imagine if the diagnosis was breast cancer. A doctor would not tell a patient to come back in six months for a check, but we see that happen with dementia all the time."

Tami has observed a huge void in education about dementia. Foremost is the general misperception that nothing can be done for it, but she believes many things can be done to combat some symptoms. She acknowledged that it is not a great diagnosis but affected people can still live a positive life.

When a person is initially diagnosed with dementia, she advises the family to push for a specific diagnosis. She believes it is important for them to get second opinions and further testing to determine exactly what disease is causing the dementia.

Next, she urges everyone who is diagnosed to find a support group. She told me there are groups for couples, called "gatherings," that they can attend together. She also said it is important for caregivers to attend a separate support group because they need answers to their questions and support from people who are going through a similar experience.

As I've noted in this chapter, caring for a person with dementia requires a lot of adjustment on the part of a family, especially the primary caregiver. Tami explained that dementia affects a person's ability to perform activities of daily living (ADLs), such as bathing, getting dressed, brushing teeth, going to the bathroom, and even eating. Through support groups and education at dementia support centers, caregivers gain tips on managing ADLs for dementia patients. As an example, a caregiver cannot place a lunch tray in front of a person with dementia and tell them to eat. That person may not know how to use a fork or may say that she has already eaten when she has not.

I spoke with Tami about the demands this level of care and attention places on a spouse or partner who is a caregiver. Tami echoed Dr. Petersen's advice about the importance of care for the caregiver. She said dementia is a long journey, and we need to help spouses through that journey. She noted that many spouses feel like a widow long before their partner dies. They live alone, eat alone, and any plans they had for the future are gone. Their life is empty and lonely, even though they are still married.

She said those in the dementia care field refer to this as "the long goodbye," and she observes that it is often also a double goodbye. A spouse has to say goodbye to the person they knew so well and embrace who that person is now. They may love their spouse as always, but the relationship is not the same.

Tami said some people begin to feel they are married to a disease, not their spouse, and that is especially true for spouses who are also full-time caregivers. The reality is that as parents, we expect to take care of our children, and as adults, we expect to take care of our parents. But most people do not expect to care for their spouses, feed them, take them to the bathroom, or have to remind them daily to do the same, simple tasks.

Tami offered advice for spouses who are caregivers. She said a person who has dementia will follow the lead of their spouse, so if the spouse is upset and frazzled, the dementia patient will be upset and frazzled. That is why she encourages caregivers to manage their emotions by taking care of themselves and finding support.

WHEN TO CONSIDER A MEMORY-CARE FACILITY

Tami said that in her work, she has seen caregivers have such an elevated level of stress that many of them pass away before their unwell spouse. She told me about a woman in a support group who lived with a husband whose dementia had made him become verbally abusive. She was utterly distraught, deeply sad, and not taking care of herself. But when she suggested to her son that her husband enter a care facility, he became angry with her. Her son did not recognize that she was in no position to care for herself, much less anyone else.

Tami has learned over the years that when dementia patients lash out verbally or physically, there comes a point when they probably need to move to a facility. She said it is almost impossible to manage their behavior and manage any type of self-care at the same time.

The other phenomenon that Tami sees is the amount of unpaid caregiving that occurs in most families. She said that she personally experienced it, as did her mother-in-law. In the United States, there are billions of dollars saved each year because family members choose to care for someone at home versus placing them in a facility. She said the reality is, if everyone who needed care was sent to a facility, the facilities would quickly be overloaded. We do not have room to care for everyone who is being diagnosed with dementia.

I asked her about getting in-home nursing care versus going into a facility. She said the reality is there are very few people, other than the very wealthy, who can afford twenty-four-hour in-home care. Tami has seen many family caregivers able to piece together care for the daytime hours, but they are still left with nighttime care. Unfortunately, oftentimes people with dementia have trouble sleeping and can wander, resulting in challenges for the caregiver to keep that person safe at night.

With in-home care being out of reach for most people, I asked Tami about the costs of a care facility. She told me there is no getting around the fact that care facilities for dementia patients are expensive. The typical cost is between $6,000 to $10,000 per month. Some facilities are owned by large companies, and some are group homes, so the expense can vary greatly. She said some people have long-term care insurance policies that can help defray some of the costs, but the financial outlay is still substantial.

Tami said the best solution for everyone involved is if a family can find a good, affordable care facility near them. There are some facilities that accept elderly patients based on their finances, and there are some that receive a stipend from the government for taking in dementia patients. That said, she acknowledged that most of these facilities have long wait lists because the need is so great.

The need for more caregivers and care facilities is only going to grow. Tami observes there are a lot of people being diagnosed at a younger age, and their needs are different from previous generations. For example, she said frontotemporal dementia usually occurs around age fifty-five, and a fifty-five-year-old with dementia has different needs than an eighty-five-year-old.

The increase in the number of people with dementia is like a tidal wave going through our population. Tami told me that, in her opinion, the care system in the US needs a lot of help and reimagining to meet the needs of the not-so-distant future. She believes that we must work to improve our system so we can better address the specific needs of all types of dementia and that the key is better education and support.

But in the meantime, caregivers must try to figure out how to provide the best quality of life for dementia patients. I asked Tami for advice on how to keep someone performing at their best for the longest possible time.

SOCIALIZATION IS IMPORTANT
FOR DEMENTIA PATIENTS

She told me that whether a person with dementia is at home or in a facility, socialization, or life enrichment, is especially important. Socialization is not medical or personal care; it is everything else that goes on in a person's daily life.

Tami recognizes that dementia is not a fun road, and it only gets worse, but she believes that there can still be joy along the way. She has found that the best way to find joy is through doing things that the person always loved to do.

She told me that if a person with dementia likes to go to the movies or listen to music, that activity should be part of their care. It allows them to have joy. That person is still entitled to live a vital life, even with dementia. She believes that activity allows the world to see that a person is still an important part of the community, even if they are in a nursing home or assisted living.

She told me, "No one wants to become the disease. Every person has rights, and I believe a person with dementia should be at the center of care, where family, care professionals, and the community meet their needs."

My discussions with Kathryn, Adele, Dr. Petersen, and Tami helped me better understand dementia and the problems that accompany the disease, not the least of which is the burden our society puts on caregivers. As the Baby Boomers age and life spans increase, our institutions will be overwhelmed. We need to improve the support available to patients and caregivers as expeditiously as possible.

LESSONS LEARNED ABOUT DEMENTIA:

- It is critical to diagnose the specific type of dementia.
- The earlier dementia is diagnosed, the better the patient and family can prepare.
- Dementia should not have a stigma associated with it—it is a disease of an organ, like many other illnesses.
- Once dementia is diagnosed, the patient and family should get legal documents in order and information about everyday tasks documented.
- Dementia patients and their families need to establish trigger points for when the patient should no longer make important decisions, sign documents, or drive a car.
- Caregivers can seek help from doctors, support groups, and community resources to cope with the mental and physical aspects of caring for someone with dementia.
- Often, the best outcome for a person with dementia and their family is to enter a care facility.
- We all need to work on improving the options for dementia patients and their caregivers.

CHAPTER SIX:
STUNG BY SUDDEN DEATH
Accidents, Suicide, and Shock

*"IF I HAD KNOWN, THE LOVE
I WOULD HAVE SHOWN."*
Reba McEntire

THREE MONTHS. THAT is all the precious time my husband, Bucky, and I had together after his cancer diagnosis. We had hoped and prayed that the chemotherapy treatments would give him more time. I felt cheated when he died so quickly.

But after interviewing widows who lost their loved ones suddenly, I came to realize that three months sounds like a gift to them. It afforded me time, albeit a short amount, to prepare myself for the fact that Bucky was dying. When a partner dies suddenly, whether it is an illness, by suicide, or an accident, the survivor had no opportunity to say "I love you" one last time. They had no closure.

I know firsthand that the death of a loved one is shocking, even when you know it is coming. But when death is sudden and unexpected, the shock is particularly acute, carrying extra emotional burdens. I learned that a sudden death brings with it complicated grief that is difficult to work through.

Before I started my research, I assumed that most widows were like me—at a minimum, they would be old enough for Social

Security. But when I learned that the average age of a widow in the United States is fifty-five years old, it occurred to me that there must be a lot of younger women who have also experienced the death of their spouse.

My daughter Kate told me about one such woman, Liz, a young friend of hers whose husband died suddenly. You don't think about a woman in her early thirties becoming a widow, but that's what happened to Liz. Since losing her husband, Liz has encountered distinct issues that most older widows do not face, so her story was sad to me in a different way. Liz has confronted her change in circumstances head-on, and her wisdom about being a young widow was enlightening.

Liz and her husband, Graham, had been lucky in many respects. They were high school sweethearts who married after graduating from college and, over the years, became parents to three children. They spent much of their free time at their Minnesota cabin, where Liz's sister and her family owned a home on the adjoining property. On warm summer days, Liz and Graham's children could run next door to play with their cousins. Her life was ideal.

During one weekend at the cabin, Graham was cutting down a dead tree on the property when it unexpectedly crashed to the ground. It landed directly on top of him. Graham died instantly. Liz was thirty-one years old, suddenly a widow with an infant and two preschool children to care for alone. The love of her life was gone without warning or time to prepare.

Even before this tragedy, Liz had been in mourning because her mother had died the previous year. That experience helped her understand the grieving process. She knew that there would be highs and lows and that sadness and pain would be her companions for a long time. She was a veteran of grief. Her four-year-old son remembered the death of Liz's mom, so he understood when Liz told him his daddy had gone to heaven and would not be coming back. Her three-year-old daughter knew that her dad was gone but had trouble processing the permanence.

A fog seemed to envelop Liz after Graham died. She thought she was present the week of Graham's death and funeral but on reflection, realized she was not. She was operating on automatic pilot, busy caring for the needs of her three small children.

Those needs were front and center the day after Graham's funeral. It was her daughter's third birthday, and her little girl was expecting a party. That morning, Liz received a text from her mother-in-law lamenting Graham's death, saying she was struggling to even get out of bed. She asked Liz if she was feeling the same way.

Liz read the text and shook her head: She did not have the luxury of giving in to her grief. She got out of bed and acted like it was the best day ever so her daughter would have a good birthday. She said, "As brutal and as hard as it's been being in charge of these three kids, it's been my major motivator to stay on track and function."

Liz looked for support from other widows but struggled to relate to those she found in online groups. Their remarks about being grateful for the time they had with their husbands irritated Liz, who was still struggling with the double loss of her mother and husband.

It has been three years since Graham died. Liz's older son, now seven, understands that his dad is never coming back and has some faint memories of him. Her six-year-old daughter's memories of Graham have come only through videos and pictures. Her youngest son, now three, looks at pictures of Graham and says, "Do I have a dad? Who is that guy?"

Liz has learned how to talk with her children about Graham. She says that if they come to her and say, "I am really missing Dad, and I am sad," they don't want or need her to tell them, "We are fine, we are so lucky." She understands that what they want her to acknowledge is that she is sad, too. She asks them specifically what they are thinking about Graham and listens intently to their response. She told me, "They just need me to acknowledge how they feel. Once we have had a little cry, they next ask me, 'Where are my Hot Wheels?'"

Recently Liz's sadness has tilted toward hope. Counseling has helped her to find that hope, providing a place where she is reassured that her thoughts and feelings are normal.

Liz is not sure what her future will bring. She is open to another relationship but observes that many of the widows she meets believe the only way to be a successful widow is to remarry. Liz does not buy that. "I would love for remarriage to happen, but if it doesn't, I want to know that I'll be fine," she said.

Soon after I spoke with Liz, I mentioned the topic of young widows to a friend. She told me about her friend, Sharon, who lost her husband suddenly. He was a young man, a father of three small children, and seemingly in good health. I called Sharon to ask if she would share her story. Like so many of the widows I interviewed, she agreed to talk with me, share the pain of her experience, and relive the trauma of losing her spouse.

Sharon's story begins on a Monday morning in February 1995, when she and her husband, Tony, were starting their normal workday routine. Sharon was in the kitchen preparing breakfast and tending to the children while Tony was getting ready for work. She heard him start the shower and, minutes later, a loud noise. She assumed Tony had knocked something over in the bathroom.

When his shower seemed longer than usual, Sharon went to their bathroom to investigate. She entered the bathroom and found Tony on the floor, no longer breathing. Sharon shouted to her eight-year-old daughter to call 911 while she performed CPR on Tony. When the paramedics arrived, no life-saving method could revive him. They pronounced Tony dead of a massive heart attack. He was thirty-seven years old.

Sharon describes the next phase of her life as "functional shock." She and Tony were so young that death was not something they expected to face so soon. Expected or not, Sharon had three children to care for, all under the age of nine. She was thankful for the routine of taking care of the children and running the household.

The shock of Tony's death was horrific, but tending to her active children kept her grief in check.

Fortunately, Sharon had the support of a loving family; they helped care for the children and sort through the household finances. She and Tony owned their house, and Tony had left her money through a life insurance policy.

But dealing with the household finances was new to Sharon. During the course of their marriage, they had little cash or investments, so she was inexperienced with budgeting and managing a portfolio. Her brother-in-law put her in touch with a reputable financial planner who began the process of educating Sharon about investments. It was stressful as she embarked on a huge learning curve, but six months later, she had a good handle on how to manage her money.

In addition to the loss of Tony, Sharon also endured the loss of her career. She had been working weekends as a nurse at a nearby hospital, but after Tony died, she had to quit her job because spending two days away from her children was no longer feasible. Her job had been fulfilling and important to her. Now it was just another loss, both financially and emotionally.

Sharon's grief began to affect her normally upbeat personality. Her sense of humor and joy for life evaporated. She went through the motions of life in a robotic trance for almost a year. She gave up drinking alcohol, though she had only ever been a social drinker. She knew it was wrong to use alcohol to numb her emotions at a time when she was already feeling numb.

She worried about how Tony's death was affecting the children. She knew they needed an outlet to express their loss, so Sharon arranged for them to attend a grief group for kids. She was not certain it would help, but she believed that it would not do any harm. The children had time set aside each week for them to talk about their grief in a safe environment, whether they chose to do so or not.

Sharon was skeptical about seeking therapy for herself but decided to give it a whirl. Fortunately, she found a therapist who was easy to talk to and helped her find a good path forward. Sharon now says she doesn't think she could have survived without it and encourages everyone to try it. Sharon also found time to exercise and began to eat a healthier diet. Her journey to self-love and well-being had begun.

Still, it was not all smooth sailing. Her two oldest children struggled with the loss of their dad when they got older. Her daughter remembers all the stress of that time, having picked up on Sharon's stages of grief. Her middle child acted out with substance abuse. The baby of the family was the only one spared because he does not remember his dad, which caused a different type of trauma. Sharon also went through a period of anger, furious at Tony for dying.

Eventually, a year or so after Tony died, Sharon regained her sense of humor and her zest for life. She was young and vibrant and knew that at thirty-eight years old, she was not even halfway through life. She met Bob, who was fun and caring and provided the emotional support that Sharon needed. They were married a few years after Tony's death.

Sharon and Bob faced many of the challenges associated with blended families. Sharon's children had enjoyed having Bob around, but once he became their stepfather, they resented his role in their lives. Their mom's remarriage exacerbated the emotions around the loss of their father. The family went through a rough patch but eventually sorted it out; Bob will never be their dad, but they have an appreciation for his presence in their lives.

Sharon still grieves over Tony, but that grief has become less acute over the years. She gets sad, especially around the anniversary of his death. "The grief does ease, but the memory doesn't," she says.

I thought it was difficult to become a widow later in life, but I learned through Liz and Sharon's stories that the burdens of being a young widow carry with them all the same difficulties, but they are magnified when you are also raising young children. My co-author, Suzanne, has a friend, Jane, who, through both circumstance and shrewd planning, was able to navigate the rough waters of young widowhood and come through it successfully.

Jane met her husband, Don, at a bar near Case Institute of Technology, where he was a student. The bar attracted intellectuals with a taste for classical music and a good martini. Don graduated from Case as a particle physicist and was a man for all seasons. After that first meeting in the bar, Jane never looked back. They were married immediately after she graduated from Ohio State. She got pregnant with their first child almost right away, and they had their second child three years later.

Don's raw intelligence made it hard for him to work for anyone he thought was less intelligent than him. Consequently, he changed jobs frequently, and Jane and Don, with two children, did not enjoy a lot of financial security.

One day, fifteen years into their marriage, Don was sitting in their backyard when he suddenly slumped over. The couple's son rushed into the house, saying, "Something is wrong with Dad!" Don had suffered a fatal heart attack. Paramedics rushed him to the hospital, but the doctors could not revive him. He was forty years old. Jane found herself widowed at the age of thirty-five with two children, aged thirteen and ten.

Jane's children were old enough to understand what death meant. When Jane broke the devastating news, she also told them they were now a team of three. "From that moment on, we were a resolute team, and they haven't stopped being a team to this day," she says. Both children learned to do a lot around the house. Her son started mowing the lawn after Don died without being asked, checking the weather and adjusting his schedule if needed.

Jane's neighbors consisted of young, married couples—no one was divorced—so Jane was the only single person. That could have been an isolating situation, but her neighbors stepped up to help her. Unlike the stories some widows tell, Jane's married friends continued to include her and her children in their social activities.

Fortunately, Don had purchased life insurance, so between that money and Jane's job, the family had enough money to take vacations and partake in lots of sporting adventures. Looking back, Jane says she was really trying to fill her life with activities and wear herself out, so she did not have to think so much about being a widow.

A few years after Don died, Jane was promoted to a project manager position at the specialty chemical company where she worked. Her life was going well, but she still felt the void of not having a partner. Jane's mother had been widowed when Jane was nine, and while she lauds her mother for being a significant role model, she knew she did not want to live the same, lonely life of her mother, who never remarried. Jane dated a bit—and was hit on by some of her friends' husbands—but was particular about letting someone into her life. She had seen many divorced friends remarry for the wrong reasons, mostly due to loneliness. "Everyone needs to learn to live alone," she says.

Despite Jane's desire to find someone new, she had also witnessed the pitfalls of second marriages. She saw her friends struggle with blending families, and she wanted better than that for her children. She was also cautious about the life insurance money Don had left them, determined that it would not be used to support someone else's children. Jane was financially secure, had good friends and a lot of professional respect. She lived a good life, alone, for twenty years.

When she was in her mid-fifties, Jane met Bill, her current husband. Today she and Bill enjoy a loving relationship with her children and grandchildren. She still feels some sadness at losing Don. When she hears one of his favorite classical songs on the radio, she believes that it is a sign that Don is watching over her. She is sorry that he never got to see his children grow up or meet his grandchildren. She believes he would be so proud of all that they have accomplished.

Jane's advice for younger women is to prepare for the possibility that their spouse will die. She cautions, "When you're young, you don't think something like that can happen. But everyone, regardless of age, needs to prepare because once your spouse dies, you just don't have the energy to face things if you have a mess on your hands."

Jane was fortunate in some ways. When Don died, her children were old enough that they understood the concept of death. They were also of an age where they were able to be somewhat self-sufficient. But Jane also made some good decisions along the way. She was wise to recognize that a blended family was not what she wanted for herself or, more importantly, her children. Although she says she spent many lonely hours, she is sure that the choices she made were the right ones for them.

After learning of the struggles these young women endured, I reflected back on the advice from the attorneys I interviewed in Chapter Two. They all advised that—regardless of age—people need to plan for a day when one spouse may not come home. But there are aspects other than potential legal complications when someone dies suddenly. How does one cope with the shock of it?

Once again, I called on Lynn Kiely, the psychotherapist introduced in Chapter One, to provide some insight on dealing with a death that was completely unexpected. As usual, Lynn provided some good information and practical advice.

SUDDEN DEATH CALLS FOR A DIFFERENT GRIEVING PROCESS

I learned from my conversation with Lynn that a sudden death, like one that occurs after an accident or lethal heart attack or brain aneurysm, is a shock to the survivors and can bring a different kind of intensity to grief. She explained that an unexpected death can bring more immediate trauma because there was no time for preparation. There is no possibility of finishing any personal business with that person.

Lynn told me that the process of grieving—where the end goal is peace for the survivor—is complicated by the shock of sudden death. Often, survivors have an unfinished feeling because they did not get an opportunity to say what they would have if they had known their partner would die. It also changes their thoughts about the future because the death cuts short any plans the couple had made. She said all of this may make the grieving process last longer, and the survivor may find it more difficult to find a sense of peace.

Lynn explained how a sudden death is different in a way that resonated with me. She said that when a couple has a shared sense of anticipated death, as with a terminal diagnosis like Bucky had, they have an opportunity to grieve together beforehand. But she said when that shared grieving does not occur, so much can get lost. In those cases, when a spouse is suddenly left alone with that internalized grief, the healing can be more difficult. Lynn said that in her experience, the patient's healing may involve more emotional, meditative, spiritual, or therapeutic work to come to some measure of peace and acceptance.

She highlighted that another problem she sees if a partner unexpectedly dies is that any unresolved issues they had may persist. The chance for reconciliation and forgiveness, even if it is a fantasy, is lost. In these cases, she said the widow may feel like a victim and mourn the death of the chance for resolution.

As I listened to Lynn speak about a sudden death, I thought about something even more complicated: suicide. I had an acquaintance, Merrikay, whose husband died by suicide, and I remembered how tragic it was. I didn't know Merrikay or her husband well, but I had admired them both from afar. She always had a smile on her face, and her husband was always at her side. They were a fun couple to be around, always the life of every party. Or at least that's how it appeared.

When I heard that Merrikay's husband died by suicide, I found it hard to believe. Many of us understand so little about suicide and even less about how to talk to someone who has experienced the loss of a loved one because of it. When I began thinking about this book, I knew that I needed to include something about suicide and the effect it has on the widows left behind. I called Merrikay to see if she would tell me her story, and she graciously agreed.

She told me she and her husband, John, met in junior high, began dating as high school sophomores, and married four years later. She said they lived a good life, complete with two sons and the traditional house with a white picket fence. For years, John was a successful business owner, and the couple enjoyed the fruits of his labor, including a condominium in Florida where they could escape the brutal Midwestern winters.

When John was in his mid-fifties, he began experiencing minor physical problems. The waning of his normal prowess weighed on him. He had a family history of depression, but he had always been a "pull yourself up by your bootstraps" kind of guy. Even as his personality became angrier—sometimes turning to rage—Merrikay chalked it up to aging, her husband becoming a "crotchety old man."

She didn't know that John was exhibiting classic signs of depression.

As he neared seventy, John's business took a turn for the worse. Technology began to replace the old-boys-club sales network he was accustomed to, and that transition had dire consequences on the bottom line. He glossed over the problems with Merrikay, only acknowledging to her that the finances weren't as good as they once were.

Eventually, John decided to sell the company and seek employment elsewhere—and the financial pressures grew. But finding a new job at his age was not easy. After interviewing for a job he thought he would get—and learning that it went to someone younger—John was devastated. He knew that he and Merrikay would be unable to maintain the lifestyle they had enjoyed for fifty-one years. He was despondent and believed that he had let Merrikay down.

That rejection triggered a reaction that snowballed and ended in suicide. On that fateful Thursday morning when John lost out on the prospective job, Merrikay now believes he just gave up on everything. He purchased a gun, drove to a remote area, and parked his car. He walked far from the car and shot himself. He left the registration for the gun and the lease papers for the car on the front seat. For three days, Merrikay was in agony, waiting to hear from John. One of her sons knew John suffered from depression and told her, "Mom, I think he's gone." But her other son was more optimistic and spent two days looking for him. Merrikay knew of his family history of depression and feared the worst.

On the fourth day after John's disappearance, a sheriff's deputy came to the house to deliver the news: a hunter had found John's body. He said, "Your husband must have really loved you because he walked far away from the car, and he was in an area where he knew no family member would find him."

Merrikay had no idea that John's mental state had spiraled so far down. She had noticed a decline in his physical appearance and upkeep, but she attributed that to the normal aging process. The night before he died, he joked with her, acting perfectly normal.

Merrikay got through the next few days and the funeral by assuming her people-pleasing personality. She felt the need to hold it together for everyone else, but she was suffering inside. And then the COVID-19 pandemic hit.

Merrikay was alone in her apartment, isolated from everyone. She spent her days in tears. She lost weight because she could not keep food down. She grieved the loss of John and questioned why she did not recognize his deep pain. She was also upset that John, who had always been a lovely writer, did not leave her a note to explain why he ended his life so she would have some closure.

When COVID restrictions eased, Merrikay accepted any invitation to socialize. Between the effort needed to put on a happy face and a lack of sleep, she wore herself down. Looking back, she wishes that she had been more honest with her friends when she was having a difficult day. She was so intent on not wanting to be the sad sack that she ignored her own best interests.

Merrikay also suffered indignities thrust upon her by people asking inappropriate questions. Questions like, "What type of a gun did he use?" or "How bad was his business?" or, worst of all, "How could you not have known he was so depressed?" Merrikay found that being the widow of a suicide victim made her the elephant in the room at any gathering. People just stared at her, not knowing what to say, and even her close friends could not bring themselves to mention John's name.

Merrikay finally sought therapy, and the counseling and guidance she received made an enormous difference. Among other things, the counselor told her that when people ask inappropriate questions, she is under no obligation to answer them. Instead, the counselor advised her to turn the tables and say, "Why would you ask me that?"

The counselor also helped Merrikay overcome her feelings of guilt about preventing John's suicide. She now understands that John probably was secretly thinking about suicide for a long time, though she had no way of knowing.

Merrikay still misses John sitting next to her on the couch every night. She finds walking into an empty home jarring. She knows that she will never completely recover from John's suicide, but she would like to feel more comfortable bringing up his name in conversation rather than thinking that it is best not to talk about him at all. She wants to bring awareness to the illness of depression and help eradicate the stigma associated with it.

For now, Merrikay just hopes to become a little happier. Her life is smaller now than it once was, and she is reconciled to that. She has made one important change already: She does not waste her time with people whose company she does not enjoy.

"I used to be a people pleaser," she said, "but I am so over that now."

If a sudden death brings about complicated grief, as Lynn Kiely told me, how does one walk through grief when their loved one was lost to suicide? How does one move on without guilt? To seek answers to those questions, I spoke with Anne Gettle, the clinical social worker introduced in Chapter One.

Anne explained that she tells the surviving spouse of someone who died by suicide that, first and foremost, they have a right to their grief. It is not lessened because their loved one took their own life. She emphasized that the surviving spouse has a right to process and feel all the stages of grief the same as anyone else whose partner has died.

She said people whose partner died by suicide also need to normalize their reactions; anything they are feeling is right and appropriate. She tells clients that the important thing about feelings is what we do with them. Anne believes these are people who need to connect with other people whose spouse has died by suicide because those are the people who can provide non-judgmental, positive support from the perspective of one who has lived through a similar experience.

Anne told me that, many times, the spouse of someone who died by suicide needs time to process the relationship itself. There is usually a lot of guilt about not recognizing the signals of depression and suicide before it happens. She said that there are some suicides that can be prevented, but that requires the person intent on suicide to be in a frame of mind to ask for help. If that person is not open to asking for or receiving help, there is no way that the spouse could have known about it ahead of time.

Anne confirmed that there is no type of grief that is better or worse than others, but suicide definitely makes the survivor's grief more complicated. She explained that in our society, there is a certain amount of judgment about suicides, and that typically gets thrust on the surviving spouse. They get asked questions about why they didn't know their partner was in such pain. That type of judgment is profoundly shaming and unhelpful to the grieving process. She stresses to her clients that the way a person dies does not define their life or their relationship. When a person chooses to die by suicide, that doesn't mean they didn't love their spouse or didn't feel loved by their spouse.

GRIEF IS NOT A LINEAR PROCESS

Anne said that many people read the book *On Death and Dying* by Elizabeth Kubler-Ross, in which she describes the stages people go through to process their own mortality. But Anne points out that Kubler-Ross was not writing about how to process the death of a loved one. Anne says people who apply Kubler-Ross's theories to a loss run into two problems. First, people look at those stages and apply them to the grieving process, and second, people think of the stages as timelines they should move through.

But, she says, the reality is the stages of grief are not stair steps—grief is not a linear process. So, someone may move through the anger stage and then six months later be right back in it. Anne said that can be especially true when a partner has died by suicide, and that's OK. Everyone needs to move through grief in their own way and in their own timeline.

I learned from Anne that all grief, especially when suicide is involved, will ebb and flow over time. It goes from causing total desolation to accepting the suicide as just another fact about the person's life. She encourages her patients to understand that the loss never stops being important, and they may never stop missing their loved ones, but the *way* in which the person died lessens in importance.

After my discussion with Anne, I better understood the complexities of dealing with grief when a spouse has died by suicide. But I wanted to know more about what advice or resources are available to help work through the unique problems associated with that type of death. I reached out to Carolyn Kinzel, founder and president of Brighter Days Family Grief Center, to get her perspective.

Carolyn was working in the real estate and mortgage industries when her business partner lost his wife and son in a helicopter crash. She watched as his life spiraled out of control; he was traumatized by the sudden death of his wife and overwhelmed trying to care for their three-year-old daughter.

She began a search for grief centers that could help him but found there was no such entity in the state. She spoke with other people who had lost spouses and found they also were floundering. They needed help with practical issues—how to file for Social Security, how to close out social media accounts, or how to deal with probate. Those mundane issues paled in comparison to finding adequate assistance in helping children through the loss of a parent.

Carolyn was frustrated by the lack of pragmatic, useful counseling available to her partner. And then her own life took an unexpected turn. She was a single mom who had not married the father of her son, but he had stayed a part of his son's life. One day, two detectives knocked on her door. They informed her that the father of her son had died by suicide. Unfortunately, her son, aged thirteen, was walking past the door as the detectives delivered the news.

It was a traumatic and emotional moment, one that Carolyn was not prepared for. She was suddenly looking through the lens of a parent who needed support for her child, and this time it was she who could not find the right resource. As she struggled to find counseling for her son, it occurred to her that it must be doubly excruciating if someone is looking for support after the death of a spouse or child. It brought back all the same frustrations she felt when she was trying to help her partner.

Carolyn told me that her difficulty in finding the best resource for her situation was both frustrating and motivating. It spurred her to establish the nonprofit Brighter Days Family Grief Center because there was no organization out there that was providing an integrated approach to grief.

LOSS IS MORE THAN GRIEF

Carolyn started our conversation by pointing out that, in her opinion, our society needs to address all the issues surrounding a death, not just look to grief counseling as the only solution. She said it is hard to sleep at night when you do not know what is coming next. Sometimes, clients do not even have time to get on the phone with a grief counselor because they must show up in court, or file papers, or get to the bank.

Frequently, she sees that the logistics related to a death become so burdensome to clients that they overtake the healing that needs to happen. People become focused on figuring out bank accounts or even how to get groceries on the table, not because they do not have money, but because they can barely dress themselves. Carolyn believes everyone needs assistance in sorting through the tasks associated with a death so they can properly grieve.

Carolyn told me it is hard to give grievers a voice when our society overlooks grief. Her observation is that we are uncomfortable with it, so we tend to ignore it. She cited cancer, trauma, eating disorders, autism, mental illness, terminal illness, and addiction, all of which have a voice in our culture that injects education, awareness, support, treatment, and comfort into their cause. Grief, she suggested, has no such voice.

She said the reality is that our society does not teach people how to communicate with grieving people or simply interact with them. Carolyn tells people seeking advice about how to approach a grieving person that it is OK to not know what to say. What is not OK is to ignore the subject. Do not walk away.

She suggests that we need to give people permission to feel uncomfortable while still being loving. "I don't know what to say, but I am here" can mean absolutely everything to someone feeling isolated, misunderstood, or hurt.

Carolyn explained that our lack of education and awareness around death, dying, grief, and trauma creates isolation for the griever. She said our media does not do a good job of fostering conversations about the importance of holistic grief support. "People just do not like to talk about it," she said. "I have watched television news broadcasts about suicides or accidents that contain no suggestion about how to best help the family, other than a GoFundMe page."

She went on to say that we must look deeper, as a community, to stop viewing grief through a financial lens. People who have lost a child tell us that their negative feelings about the lack of emotional support from a close friend far outweighed the positive aspects of a financial fund. Financial support does matter, but Carolyn points out that too often, we think that writing a $50 check is a token of support and allows us to move on. She said real support means that we stay by the grieving person, offering emotional support and compassion rather than trying to fix the problem with money.

At Brighter Days, they empower the families and individuals who come to them with skills to cope when friends avoid them or say something painful, such as, "At least you have two other kids." They educate the families on how to discuss their grief individually, and also as a family; that it is OK for everyone to cry, to have off days, or to be angry. They work to normalize emotions and then provide concrete ways for them to reflect and honor "their person" together.

RESERVE A TIME FOR REFLECTION

Carolyn offered a simple but beautiful example of finding a time to reflect. At Brighter Days, they give lanterns to grieving families on which to write their loved one's name. They can add pictures or decorate them in any way they prefer. They are encouraged to light it every night at the same time, at the kitchen table, on the front porch, or wherever it feels comfortable. That becomes the place where everyone can gather if they choose. They can be silent, they can share memories, or they can stay in their room, but they always know that, at the same time every night, they are each remembering and honoring their loved ones.

Carolyn told me about a man who came to Brighter Days whose wife had died and was left with four young children. He did not know how to talk to them about their mom. He knew that he did not want every conversation to be tearful, but he did not know exactly what to say, and felt completely overwhelmed. When he received the lantern, he made the commitment to light it each night before dinner. That became their sacred space, and it allowed all of them to authentically grieve, share, and support one another.

Carolyn echoed what Anne told me about the complexity of grief rising significantly when a suicide is involved. She confirmed that in her own situation, there had been an immediate stigma to the suicide of her son's father. She had to endure a lot of "why?" questions and her son had a rough time at school because of it. She had family and friends, but not a lot of societal support, and she believes that was due to the stigma and secrecy of suicide.

She has observed that when someone is grieving a loved one who died by suicide, it is exceedingly difficult for them to come to terms with it. There is so much emotion involved. There is anger and blame that goes both ways, for the person who died *and* the survivor.

At Brighter Days, they help people understand that the suicide had nothing to do with the survivors. The deceased person was in so much pain that they could not see any other option but to eliminate the pain.

Carolyn told me that people often associate suicide with mental illness, but that is not always the case. Sometimes people die by suicide because of the consequences of bad choices; they were arrested for a crime or were caught having an affair. In that specific moment, they saw suicide as the way to escape those consequences.

I learned something I hadn't given much thought to: religion's impact on suicide. Carolyn said that some survivors have a tough time reconciling suicide and their faith. If their faith instructs that a person goes to hell when they die by suicide, it becomes a complicating factor in their grief journey. She said that belief can change how they feel about their loved ones. They may question whether they will be reunited in the afterlife, and the survivor often is angry, feeling that their loved one "ruined" their chance to be together again. The reconciliation of suicide and faith is a tough barrier for some people to get past; their initial response to the death is anger rather than sadness, so it takes longer to work through the process.

CONSIDER TRAUMA THERAPY

Carolyn explained that it is important that people find a grief group where they can relate to the other members. For example, a parent who has lost a child to cancer has a unique perspective that differs from one who lost a child to suicide. The parent whose child died by suicide can feel guilty because they think people believe their child chose to die while another person's child was fighting to live. This is yet another mistaken belief illuminated by the stigma of suicide.

She said when a loved one dies suddenly, the surviving family members may need trauma therapy. It is important, especially for survivors of suicide victims, to go through trauma therapy as well as grief therapy. Carolyn said that a key to successful grief therapy is untangling grief from any reaction to trauma.

She said many people, especially parents or individuals who witnessed a traumatic death, have no idea that they have experienced trauma and that the trauma could have led to post-traumatic stress disorder (PTSD). These people did not receive a diagnosis of PTSD, even though they were not sleeping and were experiencing nightmares. These people may require trauma therapy to specifically address the trauma that can go along with grief. Trauma and grief are two different animals, and both deserve the proper support.

Carolyn explained that grief therapy is about what is going on in a person's heart, while trauma therapy is about what is going on in their head. Trauma is often what causes the visions, nightmares, the inability to sleep, or the triggered anxiety attacks. Trauma therapy has specific modalities, such as eye movement desensitization (EMDR) and reprocessing and accelerated resolution therapy (ART), which retrain the brain to soften a traumatic image. Both are commonly used to treat PTSD.

Regardless of how someone died, Carolyn said it is vital that survivors have at least one person who says, "I am here for you and will be with you, and we will go through this together." When they see that happen for clients, they begin to see the healing process start. She feels gratified in those moments. "One person reaching out to help another is a beautiful thing to observe," she said.

As I said at the beginning of this chapter, three months can seem like a lifetime to someone who lost a spouse suddenly. It reminded me of the adage, "I cried because I had no shoes until I saw a man who had no feet." I will always be grateful for the time I was able to spend with Bucky, saying our goodbyes and grieving the loss of his life together.

LESSONS LEARNED ABOUT SUDDEN DEATH:

- A sudden death requires a different grieving process than one that has been anticipated.

- The grieving process may take longer to go through when the death was sudden and unexpected.

- The trauma associated with grieving a sudden death is akin to PTSD and should be treated as such.

- It is useful for a family to get therapy together and for the surviving spouse or parent to also get individual help.

- A grieving person needs emotional support, not just financial donations, especially if their loved one died suddenly.

CHAPTER SEVEN: MISSING OUT ON FUNERALS AND HUGS
The COVID-19 Conundrum

"COULD YOU BEAM ME UP? GIVE ME A MINUTE.
I DON'T KNOW WHAT I'D SAY IN IT.
PROBABLY JUST STARE, HAPPY JUST TO BE THERE,
HOLDING YOUR FACE."
Pink

O N FEBRUARY 1, 2020, an ill eighty-year-old man who had traveled aboard the cruise ship *Diamond Princess* was diagnosed with a virus that was just beginning to haunt the world. He had disembarked in Hong Kong a week earlier, and the virus he contracted was a new strain of coronavirus. In fact, it was so new it was not yet officially named. Over the next few weeks, more than 700 other passengers and crew would fall ill with the same virus, resulting in 14 deaths. By March 11, the World Health Organization named the virus COVID-19 and declared it a global pandemic.

I read with interest about what was going on, but the virus and the disease it caused still seemed extremely far away. Even the name, COVID-19, an acronym that stands for coronavirus disease 2019, was strange and clinical. I could not relate it to any person, place, or thing that made it seem more real. So, like most Americans, I just assumed that it was something that would never affect me personally.

Slowly, the reality of what was happening began to hit home. The Centers for Disease Control and Prevention recommended that no gatherings of fifty or more people take place. Weddings, parades, festivals, and even my seventieth birthday dinner were canceled.

Then in mid-March, I found out that a friend who lived just a few miles away, Sam, had died of COVID. He and his wife, Bev, were both diagnosed with the disease. I spoke with Bev to learn more about her experience. I found her story to be unusual for many reasons, the most compelling is that she was one of the last women allowed to sit with her husband as he lay dying from COVID.

Bev and Sam's story started on a blind date when they were students at the University of Maryland. It was a relationship written in the stars—they even shared the same birthday. They married, raised three sons, and built a successful real estate development business. The only blip in their life was Bev's diagnosis of lung cancer. She resolved to beat the disease with her usual grit, and she did. She was determined not to leave Sam alone.

In March 2020, when COVID first appeared, Bev and Sam were happily retired in North Scottsdale, Arizona. One day, as they were playing golf, Sam began to feel sick. At first, he thought it was due to the usual springtime allergies that plague so many people in the desert. Sam told Bev to keep playing, that he would just ride along in the cart while she finished the round.

But when they got home, Sam developed a fever and could not move. Bev called 911, and the paramedics took him to the hospital—without her. The paramedics told Bev to stay back, unsure if the hospital would allow her in.

Later that night, the doctors diagnosed Sam with COVID. The hospital staff asked Bev to come in to be tested, and, sure enough, Bev had an asymptomatic case. Though she felt fine, they admitted her overnight due to her history of lung cancer.

She felt bewildered and scared. Sam had always been incredibly healthy; he exercised every morning and was trim and fit. How could it be that Sam was the one so sick?

By the next morning, Sam had developed pneumonia in both lungs. He was moved to the intensive care unit and was told he would need to have a ventilator tube inserted to help him breathe. Before they connected the ventilator, they allowed Bev to see him. As she entered the room, he called out, "Hi, babe!" and then the technicians inserted the tube down his throat.

Bev was released from the hospital that day with instructions to stay home and rest. A few days later, Sam's nurse called Bev with news that Sam's condition was worsening and she should immediately come to the hospital. "I don't know if he was the first person to die of COVID in that hospital, but he was certainly one of the early ones," she said. "I was talking to him and holding him when he died. You never know what someone knows or doesn't know when they are in an induced coma, but he was somewhat aware."

Bev told me she realizes that she was one of the lucky spouses because most families in the US were not allowed to be with their loved ones in the hospital. Just days after Sam died, the protocols in their hospital changed, and families were no longer allowed in.

Funeral planning during the pandemic proved to be challenging, especially given that Bev was still under quarantine. At the very time that she needed hugs and the comfort of friends and family, no one could be near her.

Bev planned a funeral for Sam, but due to restrictions on crowds, she could only have her Arizona family at the service. Even her two sons and their families, who live in other states, attended via Zoom. The funeral and burial were at a nearby cemetery. When friends learned of her plans, they told her they wanted to come, even if they had to stay in their cars. On the day of the funeral, more than one hundred people attended, forming their cars in a large circle around the gravesite. No one could hear what the speakers were saying from inside their cars, but Bev says that it was the warmest feeling, like a funeral in a circle, everyone giving her a hug.

Still, she said, the loneliness was there. Bev had to drive herself to and from Sam's funeral due to her coronavirus diagnosis. No one gathered at the house afterward. Her children and grandchildren wanted to come over, but she was afraid of infecting them. It had always been Sam and Bev, and now it was just Bev.

After Bev recovered from the virus, she considered attending a widow's grief group, but by then, every gathering was taking place on Zoom, and those remote meetings held no interest for her. So, she toughed it out the best way she could.

Today, she lives with a new normal. She goes out a lot to avoid having to think about her grief. She spends time with friends, playing golf and canasta, and going out to dinner. She visits Sam's grave every day to tell him she loves him, just as she did during their fifty-eight years of marriage. Little by little, she is looking forward to waking up and being happy.

Bev is not certain what the future holds for her. She may choose to date, but after such a long relationship with Sam, she is not sure if she wants to put the work into a new one. Plus, she has been surprised that living alone is not as frightening as she thought it might be. "Sam has his eye on me," she said, "and I feel like he is an angel who is protecting me." She is comforted by the belief that when she passes, she and Sam will be reunited—when the two pieces of their puzzle will finally be back together.

COVID ALSO AFFECTED YOUNG FAMILIES

Listening to Bev's story brought me back to those early days of the COVID pandemic. With very few treatments available and little knowledge about this new virus, the diagnosis of COVID was frightening. Typically, we read that older people or those with compromised immune systems were the most vulnerable, but I heard about a young woman, Pam, who lost her husband and started a Facebook page for other young widows and widowers who were similarly affected by the COVID pandemic. I reached out to her to see if she would be willing to contribute to this book, and she kindly agreed to speak with me. Her struggles with the financial aspects of losing her husband are outlined in Chapter Three. But her story is more far-reaching than just dealing with financial matters.

Pam and her husband, Martin, were parents to a two-year-old daughter, Elsie, and a four-month-old son, Graeme. Martin worked as a speech pathologist at a New Jersey hospital, performing swallow evaluations on patients who had suffered a stroke or had oral cancer. By its nature, his profession required that he work nose-to-nose with his patients. Yet, despite that proximity, he had never caught an illness from a patient. Then, in early March of 2020, Martin woke up with a cough.

People the world over were just beginning to realize that the coronavirus was spreading; when Martin started to cough, he feared that a patient had exposed him to the virus.

Neither Martin nor Pam truly thought he had COVID, but he wanted to take every precaution. He did not go to work. He wanted to get tested, but tests were hard to come by, even for a hospital employee.

A few days later, Martin developed a fever. He worried about the children and Pam, who is a diabetic, so he isolated himself in the bedroom. When he needed something, he would text Pam, and she would leave food, water, ice packs, or whatever he needed outside their bedroom door.

Pam said that eventually, Martin was tested and found to have COVID. Every day, he got worse. He was not eating, and he slept all day. When Martin and Pam were finally able to have a TeleMed appointment, the doctor told them that the disease was just running its course. The doctors assured them Martin should start feeling better soon.

But within a few short hours of that call, Pam heard Martin gasping for air. She called out, asking him if he could breathe; he did not answer. She called 911. The first to arrive were the police, who refused to enter the house. They handed Pam an oxygen tank and told her how to put the mask on Martin's face. Finally, the paramedics came, loaded Martin onto a stretcher, and carried him down the stairs. Pam mouthed the words "I love you" to Martin as they exited the house. That was the last time they were together.

For the first few days in the hospital, Martin seemed to improve, but then he took a turn for the worse, so the doctors put him on a ventilator. In the meantime, Pam heard about a nurse at the hospital who would FaceTime a patient's family and hold the patient's hand during the call. On the anniversary of the date Martin asked Pam to marry him, Pam was able to arrange for the nurse to hold the iPad in front of Martin's face so Pam could tell him how much she loved him. The nurse later told her Martin squeezed her hand as Pam was talking.

On April 29, 2020, the staff at the hospital called Pam to tell her that Martin had gone into cardiac arrest and died.

For the duration of Martin's illness, Pam had been keeping a secret: She also had COVID. She had not told Martin because she wanted him to focus on getting better, not worry about her. She was still contagious when Martin died, so despite her grief, she told her mother, sister, and other family members that they could not come to her house for fear she would pass the virus to them. Pam was not able to have a funeral for Martin.

Pam's hardest task was telling Elsie that her papa was not coming home. She sought advice from professionals about the best way to break the news. Two days after Martin died, she explained to Elsie that her papa was up in the sky but also in their hearts.

A few months later, Elsie began to act out. Pam tried to distinguish between normal terrible-twos tantrums and behavior associated with Martin's death. Pam sought therapy for both, and through that, gained skills to help Elsie work through her grief. She is now able to express her feelings, saying, "I can't see Papa because heaven is just too far away."

Like many grieving widows during the coronavirus pandemic, Pam was not able to attend any group sessions, which only added to her feelings of isolation. However, she had a friend with two young children around the same age as hers whose husband also died of COVID, and they were able to share experiences. Knowing that her children will always have allies who understand what they have gone through has brought comfort to Pam.

Pam knew that there had to be other young widows who were also affected by sudden COVID deaths. That's when she started a group on Facebook, *Young Widows and Widowers of COVID-19*, aimed at helping each other with grief. She told me, "I looked and couldn't find a group, so I created one. We now have over five hundred members! The group is restricted to people who have lost a spouse due to COVID because there are extra layers of grief with being a COVID widow." The group meets by Zoom twice a week to talk and to provide support and encouragement.

Pam still goes through rough patches, but in general, is having more days when she feels better. She is committed to being the kind of mother her children would have had if Martin had lived. She says she gets out of bed every day because of them.

Pam is cautiously optimistic about the future. She knows that Martin would want her to be happy. He had always told her that if something happened to him, he would want her to move forward, even if that meant a new relationship. She feels that if someone does walk into her life, it is Martin's doing, just letting her know it is OK.

Still, Pam struggles when she looks at her children and knows that they were robbed of so many years with their dad. And when she sees them do something amazing, it makes her sad that Martin is not there to see it. "He loved being a papa," she said. "It's hard."

THE UNINTENDED CONSEQUENCES
OF THE PANDEMIC

Pam and Bev's stories are heartbreaking; their experiences echoed by hundreds of thousands of other people who also lost their spouse to a new and deadly disease. But as we all know, COVID had an effect on everyone's lives. Perhaps none were more affected than those who couldn't get the usual and customary physician care at the height of the pandemic. It seemed as if the staffing shortages at hospitals and the overwhelming number of COVID cases put other conditions on the back burner.

Linda, who we met in Chapter Four, is just one example of someone whose husband, Stuart, died of a non-COVID medical problem during that period. Two years before the pandemic, Stuart had suffered a heart attack and was subsequently diagnosed with Hodgkin's lymphoma. He sought treatment, but by October 2019, the doctors informed him that they had exhausted all options to fight the disease.

In the spring of 2020, when the COVID pandemic was in full force, Stuart had a regularly scheduled test at the hospital. Linda took Stuart to the hospital and was driving him home afterward when they received a call from the nurse. The test results had come back and showed a blood clot in Stuart's leg and fluid in his lungs. The nurse instructed them to drive back to the hospital immediately.

Due to the overwhelming number of COVID patients, they waited in the emergency room for three hours. Finally, a nurse called Stuart's name, but due to the worry about COVID exposure, Linda was not allowed to accompany him to the exam room. Stuart was ultimately admitted to the hospital that day. Linda was not allowed to visit him, so each day, they communicated using FaceTime and phone calls. Stuart kept getting weaker. Linda told the hospital staff that if Stuart was going to die, she wanted him to die at home.

One of the doctors gave her hope, saying, "He should be able to come home in a few days." Instead, Stuart got worse. His kidneys shut down, and he was placed on a dialysis machine. Finally, it was clear Stuart was dying, and the staff told Linda she could see him. By the time Linda arrived at the hospital, after a forty-minute drive, Stuart was unresponsive. Linda spent the day with him, and that night, went home to get some sleep. The staff promised her that if anything changed, they would call.

When the nurse called that night, Linda immediately told her, "I'm on my way!" But the nurse told her there was no need. Stuart had passed away.

Linda was surprised by how calm she felt after Stuart's death; it was as if his death had released her from the years of worry and stress about his illness. She arranged for a Zoom memorial service. None of Stuart's children would attend in person due to their worry about coronavirus exposure; they were all terrified of getting it. They consoled each other via the phone, FaceTime, and Zoom. Despite the modern technology, she still felt alone. She could not get the hug she needed through a computer screen.

The online funeral service was officiated by a rabbi, and everyone wrote down what they wanted to say. Linda struggled with how to capture the essence of her relationship with Stuart, but on the morning of the service, the sun was shining, and the day dawned brightly. Within twenty minutes, she was able to write down her lasting memories of her beloved Stuart.

Linda, like other COVID widows, had to endure the loss of her spouse without the support and help of friends and family. We do not yet have final numbers on how many thousands of people are members of the COVID widows and widowers club, but the numbers of dead suggest that it is staggering. These people have suffered not only from the loss of a spouse, but in many cases, the trauma of not being there when their loved one died.

The COVID pandemic amplified the loneliness and grief associated with widowhood and created a third challenge: isolation. I spoke with Michele Neff Hernandez, the founder of Soaring Spirits, about the distinctive issues COVID presented. She was introduced in Chapter One; here, Michele addressed how her organization quickly pivoted to meet the unique needs of COVID widows and widowers.

Michele said that the COVID pandemic dramatically altered the way in which they carry out their mission of connecting widowed people with each other. When the pandemic hit, suddenly, everyone was in isolation, and there were no gatherings or in-person meetings. She observed that isolation was especially hard for older widows who were not comfortable finding an online community.

Michele told me many people who lost their partner to COVID were shellshocked. They were not just experiencing grief; they were experiencing trauma. She also saw many people who had contracted the disease themselves, so they were alone and sick, trying to make decisions for their loved ones. These are significant decisions, and many people wrestled with making the right judgment call.

She cited cases where both the husband and wife were hospitalized. The wife got better and went home, expecting her husband to follow, but instead, his condition declined, and he died. She said those widows had to deal with a lot of survivor's guilt.

THE UNIQUE NEEDS OF COVID WIDOWS AND WIDOWERS

In one of the center's group meetings, a newly widowed woman whose husband died from a heart attack was complaining about how "stupid COVID" kept her from visiting her husband in the hospital. To the COVID widow, the disease was stupid on a completely different level. That is when Michele and her team sprung into action. They recognized that people who were widowed due to COVID had unique needs and quickly formed a specific group where they could share their experiences without input from widowed people whose spouses had died from something other than COVID.

Michele told me their COVID group had to meet in a virtual environment, which was their only option given the restrictions in place at that time for group meetings. Because so many people were already communicating with family, friends, and workplaces virtually, the meetings had a feeling of normalcy. Their online gatherings were an immediate success. Michele said the COVID widows and widowers appreciated having a forum where they could talk about how painful it was to hear the pandemic discussed in a dismissive or political way. They also had to listen to people minimize the virus or bemoan not being able to travel or go to a concert.

Michele observed that the widowed people in the group expressed frustration and a feeling of helplessness, dealing with an illness where there were few answers and many mixed messages. They questioned whether COVID could have been prevented or managed in a better way. She said only widowed people who had been similarly impacted by COVID could understand their grief and anger.

I learned from Michele that one of the greatest regrets of COVID widows and widowers was their inability to be with their spouses as they were dying. Their unhappiness was exacerbated by having to conduct intimate conversations through a cellphone or tablet held by a nurse or aide. They were grateful for the kindness of that person but felt awkward trying to hold a profound conversation in front of a stranger. These were conversations, perhaps the last conversation, where the couple could express their feelings, so having to conduct them in front of a witness was less than ideal.

Michele said another unique complication for this group was when they contracted the virus themselves and were plagued with concerns about their own well-being. They told her that when they experienced physical problems, whether it was restless sleep or a foggy memory, they had trouble distinguishing between the normal fog of grief and COVID symptoms. They lived in fear that their symptoms were due to long COVID.

There were many issues Michele and I discussed, but one of the most heartbreaking to me was that people who lost their spouses to COVID experienced long delays in having them cremated. She told me many of the widowed people in their group faced these major delays because environmental requirements restricted the number of cremations funeral homes could do in a day. So, they waited months for that piece of closure, all the time wondering about the whereabouts of their spouse's body. That horrible waiting period only added to their trauma.

PTSD CAUSED BY COVID

Michele told me that she does not use the word "trauma" lightly. She said that she and her team realized that people widowed due to COVID suffered from post-traumatic stress disorder (PTSD). She explained that PTSD pulls a person back into the original traumatic experience, so the constant barrage of COVID news impacted this group on a constant basis. She pointed out that not only was COVID the main topic of every newscast and newspaper, but it also changed the way everyone shopped, dined, made appointments... everything. There was no escaping it.

Michele emphasized that if COVID widows and widowers do not address their trauma symptoms, it complicates their grief. So, Michele and her team developed a twenty-four-week program specifically targeted at addressing their issues and helping them accept that they have been through a mentally traumatic event. She told me many of them do not realize they are suffering from PTSD, and further, they do not understand the long-term effects of PTSD.

Michele's advice to people widowed by COVID is to recognize that they have experienced a trauma and to give themselves the grace they would give to someone else. She said these widowed people often struggle with guilt, remorse, and regret. Some experience survivor's guilt. Like all widowed people, they need to learn to be kind to themselves.

Michele concluded our discussion by telling me that at Soaring Spirits, the people widowed due to COVID are encouraged to acknowledge they have experienced significant trauma and to find a community of people who have a shared experience. She said knowing they are not alone is a key element to processing what they have lived through and living their best life.

After my discussion with people affected by COVID, I couldn't help but think about the long and lasting impact of the pandemic. As of this writing, there are still outbreaks of the disease and new mutations of the virus. I know firsthand the grief and sorrow that accompanies the loss of a spouse. At times, I found it all-consuming, but there were brief periods when I could escape it. People who have lost their spouses due to COVID have no such respite; the reminders of the pandemic are still with us every day. I hope that all COVID widows and widowers are able to find a support group where they are able to share their unique experiences and find the support and comfort they deserve.

LESSONS LEARNED ABOUT COVID WIDOWS:

- Many people widowed due to COVID experienced trauma, in addition to grief.

- Attending support groups or therapy meetings virtually was the only option for surviving spouses during the COVID pandemic, thus increasing their loneliness.

- The public often trivialized COVID or categorized it as an inconvenience, adding to the grief of those widowed by the disease.

- Widowed people whose spouses died from COVID could not escape the constant media attention about the pandemic, causing triggers to PTSD.

CHAPTER EIGHT:
SURVIVING THE ULTIMATE SACRIFICE
The Unique Grief of Military Widows

"I'D HOLD YOU ONE MORE SECOND,
SAY A MILLION 'I LOVE YOU'S.'
THAT'S WHAT I'D DO WITH
ONE MORE DAY WITH YOU."
Diamond Rio

A s I was writing this book, the War on Terror was winding down, and the casualty numbers were decreasing. But since the War on Terror started in 2001, more than 7,000 US military men and women have died. Many of them left behind a spouse and children.

Military spouses contend with problems many of us never encounter—they must raise and discipline their children alone, maintain a household, manage finances, and, most strikingly, live with the constant fear that their spouse will not come home.

The majority of widows I spoke with for this book had been by their husband's side as he dealt with an illness. They were provided the opportunity to get their affairs in order and to share their intimate thoughts before his death. But military widows do not have that luxury. They hear a knock at their door and are greeted by a notification officer and a chaplain, who informs them that their spouse has died in some far-off land.

Being a military spouse—and certainly a military widow—was something I knew little about. I reached out to an acquaintance, Lee Woodruff, to ask for contacts in that community who would be willing to talk about their experience. In 2006, Lee's husband, Bob, was co-anchor of *ABC World News Tonight* and was on the ground in Iraq covering the war. He was seriously injured in an explosion from an improvised explosive device, suffered a traumatic brain injury, and was not expected to survive. However, he did recover, and he and Lee were determined to help other Americans who were similarly wounded in war. Through her work with the Bob Woodruff Foundation, Lee met Bonnie Carroll, a military widow, and so much more. Lee provided me with Bonnie's contact information, and Bonnie graciously spoke with me about her experience and how she used her grief and loss to help other military widows.

Bonnie's story with her husband, Tom, started in October 1988, when a rapidly forming ice floe in Alaska trapped a family of gray whales. Without human intervention, they were destined to die. An unlikely group of people from around the world came together to effect the rescue of the whales, including Col. Tom Carroll of the Alaska National Guard and Bonnie Mersinger, a representative from the Reagan White House. Luckily, the whales were rescued through heroic efforts, but there was also a second, less anticipated, happy conclusion to the story: Tom and Bonnie fell in love, eventually married, and Bonnie moved to Alaska to start her new life with Tom. The account of the whale rescue—and Tom and Bonnie's love story—was eventually made into a movie, *Big Miracle*, starring John Krasinski and Drew Barrymore.

Bonnie's move to Alaska was just the latest in her varied and accomplished life. She had been a successful political consultant in

Washington and was selected to be a White House advisor in both the Reagan and Bush administrations. She simultaneously served in the Air Force Reserves, where she would eventually earn the rank of major. Bonnie and Tom were very much in love and enjoyed their good fortune; as Bonnie describes it, they were living a fairy-tale life. Then in November 1994, just one month after Tom's promotion to brigadier general, he was on a flight to Juneau when his plane crashed, killing all aboard.

Bonnie had more experience with trauma than most newly widowed women. She had been through extensive training in the military, employing critical stress management techniques with people who had experienced a traumatic event. In addition, she served on the board of several groups that helped family members of homicide victims deal with the trauma of losing a loved one, horrifically and without notice. So, when Bonnie learned of Tom's plane crash, her immediate reaction was that she would be able to manage it. She thought she was prepared to go through the trauma of losing the love of her life.

But that was not the case. Her fantasy of handling Tom's death with her usual calm, collected manner lasted about thirty seconds. Then the reality set in—she was losing layer upon layer of her identity. She not only lost the person she loved, but also lost her role as a wife and the connection to the world where they had operated as a couple.

"A friend of mine said it's like someone came along and erased my whole whiteboard that had been filled with our future hopes and plans," she said. "Suddenly, I was staring at a blank board and had absolutely no motivation to start filling it in again."

Bonnie sought out a support group—"her people," as she says—where she could share her feelings and learn from others. She assumed that there was an existing group to provide emotional support, networking, case management—all the services that someone newly grieving a death in the military would need. She joined (and is still a member) of the Gold Star Wives organization, hoping they could provide that type of support, but discovered their mission focuses more on legislation and advocacy than on grief counseling and support.

With no military option available, Bonnie concluded that "grief is grief" and joined a support group for the surviving spouses of police officers. But she quickly learned that the group had their own language, they were talking in police lingo, and she did not understand much of what they were talking about. She turned to another group that was for the surviving family members of people killed in a crime but found their discussions focused on perpetrators and court dates.

Bonnie also struggled with what to do with Tom's possessions and clothes. For a long time, she did not touch the shirt that Tom had thrown over the chair the morning he left for his trip. Lots of people gave her advice about when to dispose of his things, and even whether she should continue to wear her wedding ring, but Bonnie knew that when the time was right, she would know it. She disposed of a lot of Tom's possessions but gave herself permission to keep some of them, including the shirt that Tom threw over the chair that fateful morning.

Finally, after two years, Bonnie found "her people." She was able to connect with some of the widows who had also lost their husbands in Tom's plane crash. "It was like being out in the ocean, treading water, and then finally you could grab onto a life raft," she explained. Bonnie found a community in that group who understood exactly what she had been through and could speak her language and share her memories, fears, and hopes. At last, she found a safe space to rest.

Bonnie used her contacts to find out why there was no support group for surviving military spouses. She approached both the Secretary of Defense and the Secretary of Veterans Affairs to ask who was working on providing help for the surviving families of our deceased military members. She received a typical bureaucratic response: if such a need existed, the military would have addressed it. They had never seen a need to go beyond the normal death benefits and life insurance.

But Bonnie knew firsthand that there was a vacuum. She knew that there were tens of thousands of survivors out there, wandering in the wilderness alone, trying to figure it out and having no place to come together to honor a loved one and find emotional support.

Spurred on by the lack of support for "her people," in 1994, Bonnie founded a nonprofit organization, Tragedy Assistance Program for Survivors (TAPS), aimed specifically to help military widows by providing a place where they would receive the support not offered by any other service organization, the military or the government.

In the early '90s, the Chairman of the Joint Chiefs of Staff was the keynote speaker at one of the first national TAPS gatherings. Bonnie said that prior to his speech, several surviving widows and family members approached him and spoke about their loved ones with pride and pain. He saw firsthand the extraordinary people who were there and the type of support they received from one another, making connections with others who had walked in their shoes.

When he got up to deliver his speech, he said, "All day long, I've been wondering why there needed to be this type of an organization. If we had needed it, we would have created it. But now I get it." From that point on, he said that whenever there is a military death, the family would be directed to TAPS.

TAPS has contributed greatly to the military community since its inception. In recognition of that effort, in 2015, President Barack Obama awarded Bonnie the Presidential Medal of Freedom for her outstanding service.

As I outlined in my introduction to this chapter, I knew that military deaths differ from civilian ones, but I didn't quite know how. As Bonnie explained, a military widow's experience is different because their spouse's job was serving his country, and that job is unique. That uniqueness results in different impacts when they die, and Bonnie helped me better understand those differences.

WHY MILITARY DEATHS ARE DIFFERENT

Bonnie explained that a military death impacts where the widow lives, who they socialize with, and their sense of purpose. Even their children are impacted differently. Military children have grown up with military acronyms and military ID cards. They understand what deployments mean and how that impacts military life.

Bonnie told me that at TAPS, they provide a safe space and a place to remember a life lived. They shift the focus from being about the trauma and the moment of death to being about the years of the amazing and extraordinary life that were lived, a life that included selfless service to this country.

She said that widows are often advised to get grief counseling to help them through the rough patches. She has observed that most bereaved people find talking with a therapist to be a frustrating experience. The therapists have only read about grief, and they might have good academic advice, but unless they are also widowed, they do not really understand what it is to have a broken heart and the knowledge that you will never see your spouse again.

Much of the work done at TAPS is about recognizing that people grieve because they loved, and that love transcends physical death. Bonnie pointed out that we do not stop loving the person because they are no longer physically present; we continue to love them, and we redefine our relationship with those we loved who have died. They can continue to inspire us and be a presence in our lives.

To help widows mend, the workshops at TAPS focus on letting the widows know that they are not alone and that what they are feeling is a normal reaction to an abnormal event. Bonnie said that validation, and then moving into a community of healthy support, makes a dramatic difference in their healing journey. The camaraderie with other military widows allows them to slowly mend their broken hearts.

TAPS also provides workshops on women's empowerment for these women who are seeking a new meaning and purpose in their lives. Bonnie related that it is a huge topic of conversation among the peer networking groups. She noted that one of the most important peer-based emotional support groups in existence is Alcoholics Anonymous, and TAPS' peer-to-peer groups work in much the same way. In AA, a participant cannot talk to someone who has never had a drink and believe them when they say, "You'll get through this." Until that alcoholic talks to someone who is an alcoholic and is sober, the advice just is not going to resonate. At TAPS, military widows are able to speak to someone who has personally experienced the same journey, and that helps provide validation to them.

DEATH DOES NOT DEFINE THE LIFE LIVED

Bonnie told me that currently, most military deaths are either the result of a suicide, which may follow years of PTSD, or injury. She said sometimes these surviving spouses need extra help. At TAPS, they impress on them that the manner of death does not define the life lived. In fact, it almost becomes inconsequential.

Bonnie said they know that suicide comes with many complicating factors. With many losses, the surviving family members were also caregivers, which may make them feel that they could have done more or seen the signs. But at TAPS, they advise people grieving their spouse not to look at the moment of death, but at the years of the life. These were years that included service in the military, service to their country, and a calling the person had to a higher purpose. They pose the question: How should that life be honored?

Bonnie said some military widows experience a double death if they have been caring for a spouse who was physically injured. They grieve the person they were caring for, and then once again grieve the person they knew prior to the injury. The peer groups at TAPS help with this because it is a specific type of journey that only those who have been through the "double death" can appreciate.

Bonnie has had her own epiphanies about grief and loss. She said when she was at the darkest part of her grief, a friend asked her if, knowing how much it would hurt to lose Tom, she would rather have never met him.

That was a huge wake-up call for her. Of course, she said she would not have traded a moment. She just wanted *more* moments. That realization helped shift her focus from her bereavement over Tom's loss to being grateful for having the time that they did. She said at TAPS, they have a prayer that perfectly sums up that gratefulness: "Thank God for the little while." She reflects that no matter when you lose someone, nine days, nine years, or ninety years, it is never enough time when it comes to someone we love.

Today, Bonnie says that the future is still wide open for her. She recognizes that society puts pressure on a widow to move on and remarry, on the presumption that she can then forget about her deceased husband. She refers to the scene in the movie, *Sleepless in Seattle*, where the radio psychologist says to Tom Hanks, "Whether you are fortunate enough to have love in your life again does not impact what you had with the person you lost. It doesn't change it, it doesn't make it better, and it doesn't invalidate it."

Bonnie believes that it takes a long time to redefine the relationship with the person who has died and then create a new normal. Bonnie is confident that if she is fortunate enough to have love again in her life, it will not change what she had with Tom. It will not diminish it or enhance it. Her marriage to Tom was, and always will be, an essential part of her life.

Bonnie's story, and the story of TAPS, gave me a better idea of all the sacrifices military families make. I thought again about the 7,000 military personnel who have died in the War on Terror since 2001. Those deaths represent tens of thousands of family members whose lives have been changed forever. I was determined to include a widow from the War on Terror in this chapter and began a search for just the right person with whom to speak. I searched the internet and found a YouTube clip that featured Taryn Davis, the founder of American Widow Project, a non-profit organization focused on unifying, educating, and empowering our nation's military widows.

Taryn and I had a long telephone conversation, where she kindly told me her story. She was sixteen years old when she met Michael, an outgoing boy two years older than her. She was a self-described introvert. Michael was her opposite, friendly and open to strangers. Despite the differences in their personalities, they had an instant connection and began to date. Michael brought out the fun and gregarious side of Taryn. She describes Michael as an optimist; if someone told him they wanted to go to the moon, he didn't ridicule that ambition. Instead, he would say, "Well, bring me back a rock." Taryn and Michael dated through high school and attended the same college. But midway through her freshman year, Taryn wanted to figure out who she was without a boyfriend by her side, so she ended the relationship.

They didn't speak for almost a year, until Michael called her to say he had enlisted in the Army. The wars in Iraq and Afghanistan were raging, and Taryn didn't understand what drove Michael to enlist. But when he asked to see her before he left for boot camp, she agreed.

At that meeting, Taryn learned that Michael had chosen to be a combat engineer, a role that would put him on the front lines of the action. He wanted to make a difference in his own life and those of others, he explained to her. He committed to a four-year enlistment, after which he intended to pursue another career.

Taryn wrote to Michael every day of his basic training. They chose to communicate in an old-fashioned way—putting pen to paper rather than sending emails. Taryn believes that the writing experience made their relationship more real and allowed them to open up and express their vulnerabilities in ways they never had previously.

Taryn attended Michael's graduation from boot camp, where he learned his first assignment would be in Alaska. By this time, they knew they wanted to be married. So, when he was twenty-one and she was nineteen, they wed and moved north.

They enjoyed life in Alaska for ten months before Michael received orders for deployment to Iraq. He left in October 2006. Six months later, he returned home for two weeks of R&R, but all too soon, he returned to the front lines in Iraq.

Taryn said that she and Michael spoke via Skype during his deployment. She would end every call by telling him how much she loved him, and he would always tell her he was counting down the days until his return. She noted that there was a change in his tone around mid-May. When they ended their call, instead of his usual sign-off, he said, "I know you want me to come home, but I really need to be here. There are things I need to get done."

One week later, on May 17, 2007, Cpl. Michael Davis was killed by multiple roadside bombs, just an hour and a half after his last phone call with Taryn.

Taryn was devastated. She sought support to work through her grief but could not find a local support group. She knew about TAPS, but at that time, they were only doing conferences, and attending one wasn't a possibility for her.

Taryn concluded that any support group was better than none, so she signed up for a hospice grief support group. The average age of participants was sixty-five. At just twenty-one years old, Taryn felt out of place. The group members talked about how their spouses had died; all of them lost their loved ones to cancer. Taryn asked the group what they would choose between watching their spouse dwindle away but with a chance to say goodbye or experiencing a sudden death with no goodbye. They all responded they'd choose to have an opportunity to say goodbye.

The group members told her how lucky she was because she was so young and could build a new life. But Taryn didn't feel lucky. Instead of helping her, the sessions made her feel unsupported. She was an outlier and knew that she needed to act for herself and other military widows.

Taryn said, "There is an adage, 'Comparison is the thief of joy,' and when you are newly widowed, there is very little joy." She said that military widows tend to compare their new, widowed life to when their spouse was healthy and full of life. Their inability to say goodbye also contributes to their difficulty in closing their old chapter and moving on. They instantly go from their old life to a new one, without any time for transition.

Taryn told me that after her bad experience with the grief group, she was at rock bottom. But, she observed, rock bottom is solid ground to build upon. She thought about suicide, so she could be with Michael, but she was too scared to go through with it. Eventually, she understood that she would either drown in her helplessness or she would be forced to learn how to swim.

FINDING A PURPOSE

Taryn knew she needed to act. She decided to live for Michael until she could find a reason to live for herself. She began doing research about being a widow, so she typed the word into Google. The response she got back was, "Did you mean window?"

That was an "aha" moment for her. She wanted to bring the word "widow" to the forefront and redefine it into something more positive. But she didn't quite know how to accomplish that while she was wallowing in sorrow. All she knew was that she wanted to use Michael's philosophy as her guide—she wanted to start a foundation that served other people. With that, the idea for the American Widow Project was born.

Taryn said it was not natural for her to start a group; she considers herself to be an introvert. In the beginning, the events she organized would draw just five other widows. They gathered in one big house, made breakfast together, and talked about their experiences. The small size of that first group allowed her to keep the intimacy that was important to her and everyone else in the group.

Shortly after she met with that first group, Taryn was lying on her couch watching a documentary channel on TV. The documentary format gave her the idea to shine a light on young war widows by making a documentary about them. She thought that would also have the added benefit of allowing her to hear what others had gone through and how they were notified of their spouse's death. She started asking other widows she knew to take part in her documentary.

Taryn also went online to every Gold Star Wives chat page, AOL, and MySpace site to talk about her documentary idea. She did what she called "a Kevin Costner": if she built it, they would come. And sure enough, widows started contacting her. Some widows asked if they could participate, even if their husbands hadn't died in combat. Some of the servicemen had died by suicide, and others died in support roles. Taryn said she has always hated cliques, so she readily agreed to have them join. She wanted her new organization to be for everyone.

Four months after Michael's death, she began working on the documentary. She hired people to film the widows using funds she received from the military as her death gratuity, a special tax-free payment to eligible survivors of the armed services. Taryn told me it was both magical and sad to see the interviews with widows and observe how differently people dealt with their grief. People were at different stages, and they shared what they still struggled with, regardless of how long they had been a widow. Taryn told me the interviews underscored that there are a myriad of issues widows face, and there is no right or wrong way to deal with them. The widows all had stories of love, tragedy, and survival.

The film premiered in 2008 in Austin, Texas, with more than 300 widows in attendance. Taryn decided that as long as they were all in one place, they should have fun, so she organized events like ziplining and tubing down the river. They focused on living their best lives. Taryn said it was the first time many of them had experienced joy in a long time. The gathering for the premiere of the film was the point where the American Widow Project really took off. The film, and the new foundation, were also a turning point for Taryn. She was able to connect with other young widows, and it helped her to realize that neither she nor the widows she met were on an island alone.

After that first event, things snowballed for Taryn and the AWP. She did another event in Washington and a surfing event in California. Then ABC News heard about her organization and asked to broadcast a segment about the AWP on *ABC World News Tonight*. As the AWP got more media attention, more widows came forward.

Taryn has ensured that the AWP continues to help all widows in need. A perfect example of that was her reaction to the COVID pandemic. Because of limitations on gatherings, all of the in-person meetings at the AWP had to stop. Instead, they focused on providing support through the website. During that period, they noticed that COVID widows were reaching out and asking for help. Taryn explained that the majority of military widows lost their spouses in a very sudden way, similar to what the COVID widows experienced. The COVID widows needed help and reached out to the AWP for coping mechanisms and to connect with others who had experienced a sudden loss. Taryn and the AWP gladly embraced these women and provided any assistance they could to help them through their journey of grief.

Taryn is proud of the fact that the AWP Facebook page now has over 55,000 followers. Thus far, their events and services have directly impacted more than 4,000 widows. The AWP has been nationally recognized, Taryn was named the 2010 L'Oréal Woman of Worth, she was a top 10 finalist for the CNN Heroes award, one of *Newsweek's* 150 Women Who Shake the World, and she won the 2011 Diane Von Furstenberg People's Voice Award.

MOVING THROUGH GRIEF AND FINDING JOY

Still, with all of the success Taryn achieved for the AWP, I wondered how she was personally coping with the loss of Michael. I know from experience that it is easy to bury feelings of grief by busying yourself with activities and projects. I wanted to know what her personal experience with grief has been and what her current thoughts are about widowhood.

Taryn told me that when Michael was killed, some friends told her not to call herself a widow. They said it was an ugly word, and she was too young to consider herself a widow. But she told me she doesn't think that is a positive way to view widowhood—she said it's like telling someone not to embrace who they are.

Taryn's view is that she is not just a widow, but being a widow is a part of how she defines herself. She feels it symbolizes that she loved someone deeply and cared about him until his death. She believes that is true whether someone was married for a year or for forty years.

She told me that the trouble comes when people focus on the negatives that come with the word "widow." Her belief is that, collectively, the sooner we start to see the beauty in that word, the sooner we can start not hiding from the pain and grief.

As for her own journey, Taryn said she started out in complete despair. Before Michael's funeral, her mother insisted that they drive to a salon to have her hair washed. She went a month after Michael's death without a shower.

Taryn knew she needed to take better care of herself, so she embarked on a course to discover what that might mean for her. She said, "We need to define what self-care is. A lot of times, as a caregiver or a parent, we think of self-care as a shower or a glass of wine. But those are things we tend to do in the normal course of a day."

She now defines self-care as feeling in tune with yourself, and she encourages everyone to define what that means for them. For her, it means being out in nature. When asked for advice, she discourages people from turning to alcohol or drugs, as that leads them to not having control of their emotions. But she said a creative outlet, like writing poetry or listening to music, is great.

Taryn admits that she still gets overwhelmed at times with emotions, and that is when she sits on her patio in front of trees. She read books about the stages of grief and, at times, thought she was pretty far along in the process. But then she realized that the stages of grief do not necessarily happen in a sequential order. She found herself vacillating between stages, some days up, but then the next day down.

She got very discouraged and thought she was failing grief, that she must not be doing it right. She finally realized that everyone needs to experience grief in their own way and not feel like there are certain rules and steps. She said the goal is to feel joy again in a way that honors ourselves and our loved ones.

Taryn's one piece of advice for widows is not to bury their grief. She says it's OK to feel it, but don't run away from it. She acknowledges that it hurts like hell, especially at first, to have that grief and feel like you can't get rid of it. But her guidance is that the longer you sit with it, the less the pain debilitates you, and the more you start to see your strength and resilience come through. She believes that going through that journey helps to redefine who you will be in the next chapter of life.

Taryn sought therapy to help guide her through her grief, and one day, her therapist observed that when she was giving a speech and talking about Michael, she smiled. Taryn admitted that right after Michael died, she felt guilty if she found any sort of joy or happiness, that people would think, "She's fine, she's over Michael, and she's OK." She correlated joy with being over Michael.

She didn't want anyone to think that; she still needed people to talk about him. She needed to sort through all the feelings that came up at random moments, but most importantly, Taryn wanted people to know she still loved Michael.

Today she realizes that when she is showing and embracing joy is when she feels Michael the most. She feels his presence and feels connected to him in those moments. She knows that every beautiful thing in her life she feels more intensely due to Michael's death. Taryn told me that because Michael isn't here physically to feel it, she wants to feel it for both of them.

Taryn didn't think she would ever date again after Michael died. She was happy to travel and work on the AWP. She completed some of the bucket list items that she and Michael had planned to do together, but she also created new ideas about what she wanted to experience in the future. She found a lot of happiness in doing those things on her own.

Taryn told me that she had people tell her, "I can't wait until you're happy again," and she realized they were saying that because she wasn't in a relationship. She firmly believes that people can find happiness after a loss, and that doesn't mean they have to find it in another person.

And although Taryn wasn't seeking a new relationship, she feels she was fortunate to find happiness again with a new partner. She is now engaged and has a beautiful daughter. She made clear that she didn't seek happiness in that new relationship or in having a child. She knew she had already found an ability to be happy again without them. That path to self-discovery was something that she had found on her own. Now, she told me, she is able to bring that happiness to her new family.

RELISH THE PERFECT AMOUNT OF TIME

Despite her new relationship, Taryn wanted to make clear that Michael is still in her heart. Michael is a big part of her life and always will be. She hears people say that if a widow is remarried or in a serious relationship, then they're OK. For her, she still wants to talk about Michael. She still cries on anniversaries and struggles with his death. She believes that will be true for her lifetime. She grieves for what Michael cannot experience but realizes how blessed and lucky she was to have the life she has now.

Taryn told me she could never use Michael's death as a reason for being unhappy. She said he doesn't deserve that. She still loves him and feels that if she used his death as a reason to have hate in her life or to wish part of it away, it would be as if she wished *him* away.

Taryn's outlook is inspiring. She said that instead of feeling cheated that she and Michael weren't married for long, she likes to think that they were married the perfect amount of time. She concluded by telling me, "I've been a widow long enough now that I've learned there are two ways of looking at things: the bad part or the good part. I choose to be grateful for all the good parts I had with Michael."

Before my conversations with Bonnie and Taryn, I had assumed the military looked out for surviving spouses and their children for a lifetime. I learned that was not always the case. Now, because of brave and enterprising military widows like Bonnie and Taryn, more compassionate and comprehensive programs exist for the surviving spouses of those who paid the ultimate sacrifice.

LESSONS LEARNED ABOUT MILITARY DEATHS:

- Military deaths are unlike others because the loss affects housing, children's education, social connections, and support structures.

- Due to the unique nature of the military life, it is important to find a support group specifically focused on helping widows of military members.

- It is important to shift from remembering the traumatic moment of death to focusing on the extraordinary life lived.

- Instead of thinking about the lost future together, try to embrace the concept of having had the perfect amount of time.

CHAPTER NINE:
DON'T DRINK AND GRIEVE
Alcohol's Role in Delaying Grief

"MY HEART IS DRENCHED IN WINE."
Norah Jones

L AST YEAR, I was in an examination room at my ophthalmolo-gist's office when the doctor walked in, visibly upset. I asked him what was bothering him. He shook his head and told me that he had just sent a woman home because she was drunk. She was a longtime patient in her seventies who had recently been widowed. I was shocked, but he told me that he sees it all the time—older women who are suddenly alone and unable to cope.

That conversation made me wonder how many widows there must be, navigating life on their own for the first time and using alcohol to get through the day. I thought about a friend's advice in the early days after Bucky's death to be careful with drinking. She said it was common for her clients to go from having a drink with their spouse to watch the sunset to downing a bottle before bed just to get to sleep.

It was hard to get widows to talk about their stories, and I knew it would be especially hard for those who were also battling alcoholism. The connection between widowhood and alcoholism is not a topic many people want to discuss. It is a huge problem, a secret problem, and a struggle that few widows have addressed.

Luckily, there were two brave women who agreed to speak with me, Robin and Jeanne. Their stories are quite different, but the problems they face are similar, sad, and ongoing.

I spoke first with Robin, who told me that her husband, Jason, was diagnosed with metastatic esophageal cancer at the age of fifty-one. He died six months later. Robin was thirty-two years old, with four children under the age of fifteen, and was co-owner of their family business. She had struggled with addiction issues since her early twenties but remained sober for most of her marriage.

The stress of Jason's illness caused Robin's sobriety to lapse. She became his primary caregiver and watched helplessly as he changed from a loving husband to someone who was cruel and constantly mad at her. Jason was angry at life, and Robin was a convenient target for that anger. To compound the problem, Jason, who had previously been an amazing dad, lost all patience with the children and would verbally lash out at them. Robin struggled as she alternated between protecting the children and caring for Jason. Alcohol became her escape.

Robin soon realized that her drinking was making everything worse. Jason knew she had relapsed, making him even angrier. She tried abstaining for a couple of months, but that did nothing to abate Jason's ire. She was damned if she drank and damned if she didn't. So, she drank.

She told me that at night, after a long day of looking after the business and taking care of Jason and the children, she settled in with alcohol once they were all in bed. After a while, she also began using pain pills because they were easier to conceal.

When Jason died, Robin stayed sober for seven weeks. She said she wanted to focus on her children and make sure that she honored Jason with a dignified funeral service. It was also toward the end of the year, and she worked hard to make Christmas as festive as possible for her children.

But on December 29, once the Christmas celebrations were over, stress and pressure once again overwhelmed her. She needed to numb the pain. She began drinking again, and this time, it was worse. She was drunk for three weeks straight.

Robin said her in-laws and her parents knew that, once again, she was having problems with alcohol. They took the children into their custody so they wouldn't see her struggle. With her children gone, Robin hit the depths of despair. She was convinced that she was never going to get better and that she was not capable of living a good life without Jason as her partner.

But in truth, Robin was capable—and strong. She said she finally realized that her drinking was making her miserable, so she took the bold step of checking herself into an inpatient treatment center.

Today, Robin is not drinking, but the fear of sliding back into alcohol is always with her. She is still sad about Jason's death. She is trying to work it out on her own; therapy holds no appeal for her. She is still grappling with regret that she did not make better choices in how she managed the stress of Jason's illness. She wishes she could have been more present for him, her children, and for herself.

Robin is not sure what her future holds. She is active in her church, and that provides some structure for the family. But she is still trying to navigate being a young widow, owning a business, and raising four children by herself. Her three-year-old still asks, "When is Jesus going to bring Daddy back?"

Robin's story is both sad and hopeful, and I commend her for coming forward so other women may benefit from her experience. I know from speaking with many people off the record that alcoholism is a problem, and it is increasing, but people are afraid to talk about it.

In order to gain a better perspective of the problem of widows suffering from alcoholism and learn what help is available, I spoke with Andrea Bruner, who was the director of the National Center for Women's Recovery at The Retreat, an educational recovery center in Wayzata, Minnesota. The Retreat is a supportive, educational recovery center, and many people who have attended its programs have received the help they needed to recover from alcohol and drug dependency.

I learned from Andrea that there is a well-established social stigma relating to alcoholism in women, particularly as they age. She said there is little, if any, research regarding this demographic, and therefore, it has been, and remains a hidden population. Andrea told me that the people who are seeing these women are emergency rooms, undertakers, and if they're lucky, treatment centers.

Andrea has observed that women who drink alcoholically often do so to numb emotional pain, which renders them incapable of grieving. Typically, they do not join formal grief groups or other support services. She said by the time these women get to The Retreat, they have some grieving that they need to do before they can heal. Grieving is an especially important part of succeeding in recovery.

GRIEVING IS PART OF RECOVERY

I was interested to learn from Andrea that, in many cases, grief can be caused by a more ambiguous loss than the death of a spouse. She told me that usually, there is a tremendous amount of loss that has occurred in a woman's life before she gets to the point of asking for help. For example, children leave home, parents die, friends move away. Widowhood often brings these losses to a head.

She noted that most widows are very raw. Their ability to settle into the program is in some ways challenged by the fact that they are older, may have spent fifty years in a marriage, and now they do not even know who they are. So, they drink.

Andrea said the pain these women feel is palpable because they have done no real grieving, so there is no healing that has started. She explained that what they have done is "the hop over" by taking that drink. They think they can numb the pain of grief with alcohol or drugs, but once they have sobered up, the pain persists. Using alcohol to deal with the pain of life normally does not start with the death of a spouse, but it does rapidly accelerate it.

Andrea explained that, in general, feelings are a problem for alcoholic women, so the deep feelings associated with becoming a widow are more troubling. Because alcoholism is a progressive disease, over time, she said the alcoholic widow will only get sicker.

Andrea made clear to me that she sees a difference between alcohol use and alcoholism. She told me that many people use alcohol in a way that is not harmful, but alcoholics become dependent on alcohol to deal with the vagaries of life. And then, she said, there is the physical dependence on alcohol, when the body itself starts crying out for this substance just to be able to function.

In these cases, Andrea says what has happened is the disease of alcoholism has replaced the person. Those around that person, be they parents, friends, or children, often find it bewildering because now that person is behaving in ways that are not consistent with the person they know.

Another problem is that some women are in the full grip of alcoholism *before* their husband dies, which creates more complexity to the grief. Andrea told me that when a woman is an alcoholic, there is a constant preoccupation with drinking, dealing with the incessant cravings, and then the inevitable hangover. Her life becomes consumed by this cycle, so the disease is managing her life and relationships—including her marriage.

I asked Andrea if there is a tipping point that can nudge a woman to get help. She told me that, sadly, not all alcoholics want to get help. Older women who are widowed tend to focus on their losses and cannot imagine a future that is worth the effort of recovery. But Andrea's advice is that everyone should seek help. If they do not, they often fall into behaviors that are increasingly more destructive. She has observed that most alcoholic widows tend to make self-defeating choices. They are drinking alone, and they just go deeper into their alcoholism. They become invisible to the world.

Andrea told me that if a widow is actively addicted to alcohol or mood-altering chemicals, she first needs to understand that she cannot deal with her underlying problems while being under the influence. She said if they are drinking or using drugs, they are not thinking about the underlying problems. They are only seeking oblivion and escape, and that only numbs them; it does not solve anything.

PROPER TREATMENT AND SUPPORT ARE THE KEYS TO SUCCESS

When Andrea is working with someone who has suffered a recent loss, or even an older loss that has not been grieved, she encourages them to stay in treatment longer. She explained that it takes people at least thirty days just to clear up mentally. In the next thirty days, they begin to experience a spiritual awakening that makes the vision of a new life grounded in recovery a possibility.

Andrea said there is no silver bullet to healing; nobody gets into recovery without experiencing some emotional pain. But she told me The Retreat provides a safe place for the woman to fall apart and to share her pain when she is ready. She said it is amazing to watch these women, who have been absent from their own lives, start to connect with themselves and start to show the world who they are.

Andrea admitted that not everyone succeeds in their sobriety. She said the truth is there are women who leave The Retreat and go home and start drinking again. But out of every ten women who attend their programs, six will experience long-term, contented sobriety. Those are the women who are willing to lean on other women, who are also in recovery, to form solid friendships and become part of a caring community. Andrea noted that the successful experience of overcoming addiction becomes a renaissance for the women, and that can occur even at an advanced age.

I was heartened after my discussion with Andrea to know that such places as The Retreat exist to help alcoholic widows overcome their pain and sorrow through therapy and peer support. As Andrea pointed out, many widows are able to overcome addiction and remain sober, even during the worst of times. The second woman I spoke with, Jeanne, is an example of just that.

Jeanne is a recovering alcoholic, but she has gone through periods when her strength against alcohol addiction was tested. One of those periods came unexpectedly, when she and her husband, Robert, took a sightseeing trip to the Czech Republic in 2017.

Jeanne said they had hired a tour guide and driver to visit the historical sites in the area. On a busy street near Prague, their driver turned a corner, unaware of an oncoming truck. The truck slammed into their car, instantly killing Robert. Jeanne was critically injured, with broken ribs, a smashed pelvis, and a damaged kidney.

Their three children immediately flew to the Czech Republic, and after two weeks in the hospital, Jeanne was able to fly home with them on a medical transport. She spent months in rehabilitation before she could regain her life at home.

Jeanne told me she has been attending AA meetings since 1993. When we spoke, I asked her if she was tempted to resume drinking, given the tragic turn in her life. She said she had given some thought to being a widow through the lens of being an alcoholic and how AA helped her get through her rough patch.

Jeanne said one of her greatest lessons during her time in AA was realizing that a drink will only make things worse. She has observed many women moving in and out of the program, trying to experiment with drinking, and failing. So, when the accident happened, she knew that drinking again was not an option for her.

As the weeks and months went on and she was sitting alone in her living room, it would sometimes cross her mind to have a drink. After all, no one would know. But her core belief that alcohol would only worsen her sadness helped her remain sober.

Jeanne is a firm believer in a twelve-step program, which encourages honesty, humility, and acceptance, among other sometimes challenging qualities. "In AA, you work the program, and I just wish the entire world could work it. Right from the beginning, even though I was in grief, I was able to be grateful," she told me. Remarkably, Jeanne does not feel any resentment toward the driver who pulled out in front of that truck. She abides by the credo that alcoholics cannot live with resentment. "You have to accept what's real and try to find gratitude and joy, even if it's just a tiny drop. Every day there is something to be grateful for."

I am grateful to Jeanne and Robin for stepping forward to tell their honest and inspiring stories. I hope that more people will speak out about the nexus between widowhood and alcoholism. It is a problem that is growing and needs to be addressed urgently. The aging of our population means our society is facing a spike in deaths over the coming years and, potentially, a concurrent spike in alcoholism.

LESSONS LEARNED ABOUT WIDOWHOOD AND SUBSTANCE ABUSE:

- Acknowledging past and present grieving is an important part of substance abuse recovery.

- Alcohol and drugs can mask who the person really is—both mentally and physically.

- Widows who abuse either alcohol or drugs often make bad choices, which can lead to a downward spiral of their life.

- The underlying problems associated with widowhood cannot be addressed until the person is sober.

- Alcoholics cannot live with resentment; it is important to find gratitude in something each day, no matter how small it is.

CHAPTER TEN:
EASING THE TRANSITION
Guidance to Accepting Death

"ALL THINGS MUST PASS,
ALL THINGS MUST PASS AWAY."
George Harrison

WIDOWS' LIVES CHANGE in an instant when, in one brief, horrible moment, they turn from loving spouses to grieving widows. The finality of death can leave a surviving spouse feeling unmoored and panicked, regardless of whether or how long they have known that instant was coming. I discovered a universal truth while researching this book: Most people do little to prepare for that "instant." I should know; I was one of them.

When my daughter, Kate, visited us after Bucky's diagnosis, she suggested I hire a death doula. "A *what*?!" was my response. I chalked up her suggestion to millennial mumbo jumbo. But as it turns out, she was seeing what Bucky and I could not: Bucky did not need doctors telling him to keep fighting; he needed someone skilled in guiding him through the final stage of life. We both needed help in accepting the reality of what was happening to him and to help us process the experience.

We did not take Kate's advice. I wish we had.

Looking back on the three months of his illness, I wish we had spent that time coming to terms with the end of his life rather than fighting a losing battle.

I know from speaking with other widows that I am not alone in my regret about how Bucky and I spent our final days together. Convinced that there must be a better way, I set out to explore the profession of death doulas, also known as end-of-life doulas.

I learned that the use of doulas during childbirth is common but using one for the dying process is less widespread. So, it was important to speak with people who have used one to get some first-hand perspective. Two people, Julie and Jason, were kind enough to spend time with me and explain how an end-of-life doula eased the dying process of their loved ones.

I was referred to Julie by one of the doulas I spoke with to research this subject. Julie's husband, Jay, had died, and Julie credited the use of an end-of-life doula with helping them both process the reality of his looming death. I spoke with Julie by phone and learned a tremendous amount about how a doula can make a horrible situation just a bit better.

Julie told me that Jay had always been a robust and healthy middle-aged man. So, during his annual exam, when his doctor told Jay there were some irregularities in his blood work, he assumed it was something minor. But further testing indicated otherwise—Jay had aggressive kidney cancer. Jay had never complained of any aches and pains, so both he and Julie were stunned by this fatal diagnosis.

Julie said their initial response was to fight back and beat the disease. Jay began chemotherapy infusions, but the treatments caused harsh side effects and left Jay exhausted. After two months of chemo, Jay was miserable. He vowed to live whatever time he had left as fully as possible, and that meant discontinuing treatment.

Jay's doctor suggested hospice care, but within a week, Jay and Julie knew that was not the right answer for them. They found the hospice approach to be an extension of the hospital: drug-related and not spiritually connected.

What they sought was a more personal and family-oriented care system, one that could help them determine how Jay's last weeks would unfold. As it turned out, Julie had a good friend, Janet, who was studying to become a doula. Julie asked Janet if she and Jay could become her first clients, and Janet readily agreed.

Janet began by talking with Jay, listening compassionately to what he was feeling. He knew that he was dying. He told Janet that he was on "that boat," and he believed that the family members who had predeceased him were waiting for him on the shore.

Julie, on the other hand, pushed away the thought of Jay's death. His illness and diagnosis had happened so quickly that she had not processed it. She kept thinking that they had more time, that they were going to figure it all out. Maybe there would even be a new, effective treatment.

Janet held long conversations with Julie, talking about the stages of death to help normalize the process for her. Finally, for the first time, Julie accepted that Jay was dying. She embraced the idea that Jay's passing was another milestone they would experience together.

Jay died three months after his diagnosis, on a freezing day in the middle of the COVID-19 pandemic. Julie held a Nordic wake to honor Jay's Scandinavian heritage. Julie placed Jay's body on the front porch and invited friends to come say goodbye. The next day, when the funeral home came to retrieve his body, the family carried him out. Without Janet's guidance, Julie says she could not have envisioned such a meaningful ritual.

Julie is grateful that she had Janet to lead her through the last weeks of Jay's life and grapple with the difficult reality that she needed to let Jay go. Julie believes Jay's death was peaceful, and she attributes that solely to Janet's wise doula guidance.

After my conversation with Julie, I wished that I had been able to speak with her before Bucky and I got his diagnosis. I believe her story would have helped convince us that there was a different way to approach the end of his life.

The second person I spoke with about using a doula was Jason. I read Jason's story when I was researching death doulas. There was an article on the internet where he spoke about losing his husband and how much a death doula had helped him get through that horrible period. I've never met Jason in person, but after talking with him and hearing his story, I feel like he is an old friend. Jason eloquently shared his experience of navigating his new life as a single parent and doing it all as a gay man in the public eye.

Jason told me that he and his partner, Chris, met at an AIDS Walk in Detroit when they were in their twenties. Jason recalls there was instant chemistry between the two. They made plans to get together, and following that first date, they were rarely apart.

Eventually, Jason and Chris moved to Columbus, Ohio, where Chris became the chief meteorologist at a television station. They married and adopted two children. Chris was a public figure, so the couple became a very visible example of how to navigate a successful gay marriage.

Twenty-three years later, in 2017, they were living a full and happy life when Chris was diagnosed with acute myeloid leukemia. His doctors initially recommended chemotherapy, but Chris' heart and kidneys were already failing, ending any option of further treatment.

Jason told me, "I am a man of traditional faith. So, if you had told me I needed a death doula, I would have balked at that notion." But luckily for Jason and Chris, their close friend and neighbor, Donna, had training as a death doula. Their loving friendship made it easy for Jason to invite her over and confide his feelings to her.

Jason and Chris continued to use the services of their pastor and hospice, but Donna provided clarity that the other professions could not. She was a calming and reassuring presence. She asked them their thoughts about Chris' diagnosis and allowed them to talk through the reality of their situation together, an important process that many couples avoid because they are holding onto hope or fear the conversation may upset the other. Her non-judgmental questions and advice helped them prepare for their ending as a couple and a family.

As part of their discussions, Donna suggested that Chris write a letter to Jason and the children to express his feelings for them. Chris was a little intimidated by the task, but Donna facilitated it by guiding him through a series of questions and recording his answers. He was so weak that Donna transcribed the letters for him and later provided Jason and the children with both the written letters and Chris' audio tapes. Jason said those are now among his most treasured possessions.

Jason said his experience of using a death doula has changed his feelings about death. After sessions with Donna, he now embraces the fact that death is coming to all of us, and that it is a natural part of life, just like being born. He has experienced firsthand the peace that can be reached with the help of a doula.

"I think hospice is amazing at the end of life," he reflected, "but the interesting thing about working with a doula is that it's not medication-based and has nothing to do with physical care. It's about emotional care and coming to terms with dying, and that is a very worthwhile endeavor."

Julie and Jason's stories were enlightening and only reinforced my opinion that death doulas can provide a calming transitional service that more traditional end-of-life counselors, like hospice workers or mental health professionals, might be unable to offer. I wanted to learn more, and, luckily, I was able to find two experts: Anne Murphy, the community death educator introduced in Chapter One, and Jane Whitlock, an end-of-life doula. They both assist people through the final stages of life, lending comfort and knowledge to both the dying person and their loved ones.

I spoke first with Anne to gain a better understanding of why the concept of death is so difficult for most people to talk about. She told me that, in her opinion, Western culture has become severed and disconnected from the realities of death, which is why we see denial and resistance to the death process. She pointed out that we are a youth-oriented society, and we are barraged with advertising about how to stay young and relevant. The conversations that we have are focused on life and living, while death just gets brushed aside and avoided. But, she said, life and death are two sides of the coin, and we cannot have one without the other.

Anne told me, "When I started doing this work ten years ago, people told me that nobody wants to talk about death. I do not believe that is true." She said she believes that people are curious about what their choices are, and many want to play an active role in their dying and death. These are the people now interested in having a doula.

Anne said that in her experience, she sees death being reimagined, reclaimed, and as something that we can get invited into. Regardless of how anyone dies, they are teaching us something. It can be a really challenging lesson, but they are showing us something—how to do it or how *not* to do it.

CHALLENGES BRING LIFE LESSONS

Anne explained the reality is that very few of us learn lessons when things are good, and life is fun. Instead, we learn things when life is challenging and hard. There are many kinds of death over a lifespan: a child goes to college, you leave a family home, you change a career or lose a friend. She said these small deaths are a way to prepare you for the end of life, and we should be using those lessons as a dress rehearsal because, eventually, your life is going to cease to exist.

Anne observed that oftentimes we disengage in these moments when we really should lean into them as learning opportunities. She said sometimes people wait too long to really see the truth of their illness or the trajectory of their life. Doctors often will not speak to the reality of that, and spouses do not know how to have those discussions. Frequently, the dying person refuses to have those conversations and that adds to the mystique surrounding death.

Anne also touched on a subject that isn't often considered: the high cost of dying. She confirmed that it is not unusual for people to go bankrupt because of funeral costs. She has seen people become victims of unscrupulous funeral homes because there was not an educated and informed plan in place before the spouse died.

She said the amount of money made off someone dying is staggering—taxes, funeral homes, burial expenses. She advises that it is important for us to treat our decisions about funeral and burial plans the same way we do any major decision we make throughout our life. She believes that when people have the right information, they can act from a place of their own truth and choose options that reflect their beliefs and values.

She summed up our discussion by saying, "We are consumers in life, and we should be consumers in death."

My daughter, Kate, who had encouraged Bucky and me to hire an end-of-life doula, is the person who led me to the second doula I interviewed, Jane Whitlock. Kate had seen her on a TED Talks segment and was impressed by her approach to helping people in the throes of the dying process. Jane is a trained end-of-life doula with Doulagivers in New York City. As an end-of-life doula employed by a skilled nursing facility, she often helps patients who have no family members or friends to be with them at the end of their life. She was gracious in giving me a phone interview and telling me more about her own journey and how she views the ways we handle the end of life.

Jane and her husband, Rob, were married for more than twenty-five years. One summer, he developed a cough that Jane brushed off as insignificant, but it never went away, and he became more fatigued. The doctor performed a scan and found a tumor in his kidney. More tests followed, and the doctor finally diagnosed Rob with a rare, terminal kidney cancer.

For the duration of Rob's illness, Jane said she felt like she was on a hamster wheel. She experienced no moments of peace or calm. She now wishes that someone had been there to take her by the hand and tell her what to expect, but there was no guidance, and she was left to experience that time in a panic.

Rob died two months later, on Christmas Day. Jane says she never saw the signs of his imminent demise because she was frozen with anxiety.

Today she understands that during an extraordinary time, she was stuck in ordinary time, focused on work concerns and household upkeep. She realizes that the time around someone dying is not ordinary. That time is sacred.

Following Rob's death, Jane focused on her two children, started yoga classes, and spent her evenings watching videos of her family. Most nights, she cried a lot until she fell into what she termed "the sleep of the dead." That was her first year of grief.

By the second year, Jane knew that she needed to find a new path. She volunteered in hospice and cleaned houses to make a living. A woman she worked for nominated her for a TED Talks segment and to her surprise, she got it. That talk led to her becoming an end-of-life doula and changed the direction of her life.

I started my conversation with Jane by discussing how death is perceived in our culture. She reflected that we have almost become scared of death and dying. She told me that 150 years ago, people died at home. Back then, we were accustomed to seeing dead people, washing their bodies, building their coffins, and digging their graves. We did not outsource any of it, and we grieved with each other. But, as Jane pointed out, that does not happen anymore.

Jane said there are a couple of major reasons for that shift. First, industrialization caused families to move apart, so younger people did not see their elders die. Second, when morticians began marketing embalming as the best way to care for loved ones, that began the growth of the funeral home business. Since we cannot embalm people at home, we transitioned to funeral homes coming in to pick up the body and do everything for the deceased.

Hearing Jane explain how our culture is disengaged from the dying process helped me understand why I was so reluctant to ask for help when Bucky got sick. I thought my only options were further medical intervention, or perhaps hospice. In fact, I did have hospice in for the last two days of Bucky's life, but by then, there was little they could do to help either of us. I told Jane that we had floundered during this period and asked for advice on how someone could handle things better than we did. She told me that the biggest missed opportunity in the dying journey is not engaging palliative care early enough.

ARE YOU EXTENDING LIFE OR EXTENDING SUFFERING?

Jane explained that for people to make decisions about treatment options, they need to have a clear idea of the costs versus benefits of each option, whether that is a doula, hospice, or some other service. She emphasized that you must have your eyes wide open to what is extending life and what is extending suffering.

Jane said the best time to start working with a death doula is when someone receives a serious diagnosis. That allows time for a relationship to be established. The doula can then also function as a sounding board for every treatment choice that comes up. There will be many decisions a person or couple will not have experience in making, but a doula will ask the right questions so people can identify what is important for them. A doula can help them talk through the issues they're facing. As a doctor once told her, "Listening IS palliative."

Jane told me that one of the greatest benefits of a doula is that as death approaches, a doula can assist in prioritizing the time a person has left. She has observed that when people are dying, they often have worrying thoughts that keep them up at night. It is helpful to have someone who asks them what those thoughts are and help to develop solutions for them. She reflected back on her own experience when Rob was dying. She said she doesn't think she ever asked him what worried him. Having learned from that experience, Jane now asks that question of every person she works with. She said she can help them talk through their issues; she may not be able to solve the anxiety, but she believes having someone to talk about it with is helpful to them.

She said that part of aiding a dying person is advising them to listen to their own instincts about what makes sense for their situation. Her advice is for them to be smart and not hand over all their power to the medical doctors because sometimes they have blinders on. She has read a study that says the longer you have a relationship with a doctor, the less good they become at predicting how long you might live. She concluded that sometimes the doctor puts on rose-colored glasses, too.

So, Jane tells people not to put all their eggs in the doctor's basket. Instead, she tells them to put one egg in that basket but put the most eggs in their own basket. She also emphasizes to her clients that they trust their own intuition. She cautions them not to let fear drive the bus. She said most of the time, our intuition leads us in the right direction, but many times we override listening to our own instincts.

RESPECT THE WISHES OF THE PERSON WHO IS DYING

I asked Jane about how to best support a partner who is dying. She said, "Let the person who is dying be in charge." She gave me an example of a woman whose husband was dying, but he kept getting treatments to please her. He was done, but she was not. She said partners need to have respect for the wishes of the person who is dying, and they must work really hard at accepting death. Jane acknowledged that it is not easy to focus only on what the dying person wants, but it is the greatest gift you can give them.

In her experience, Jane said the moment clients turn toward death is the moment when everything changes. They become their most vulnerable selves, they have conversations they have not allowed themselves to have, they forgive people, they say they are sorry. She said this change allows a dying person to heal wounds that have been festering for a long time. But if the person misses that sweet spot and keeps getting treatment, by the time death is staring them down, it may be too late.

To focus on what each client needs, Jane says she always poses questions to the dying person to find out what matters to them most. What type of support do they need? What do they want the room to look like? Who do they want in that room? Do they want music? She has heard a birth doula describe when a woman is in the middle of giving birth, she is in a river full of hormones, and she needs to stay in the middle of the river to be able to do her job and give birth.

Jane believes there is that same phenomenon when someone is dying; they are also in a river to do the work of dying. It is challenging work, and the doula can be there to protect the dying person so they can do their work. A doula can also educate the family about the role they play in protecting the dying person's experience.

We wrapped up our conversation by talking about what happens to the spouse or family after the family member has died. I asked her if an end-of-life doula can continue to be of assistance after the client has died.

TWO KEYS TO GRIEF: FORGIVENESS AND PERMISSION

Jane told me that she is always there to support the family. There are a lot of emotions after someone has died, and regret is one of them. She said that she views regret as a natural part of grief. She told me, "I don't think anyone who has been through this isn't overturning every stone thinking, 'What could I have done better? How could I have fixed this?'" She believes that regret is the brain's natural response to trauma. But she counsels that, at some point, clients need to let themselves off the hook because everybody feels this way.

Jane tries to educate people about the time after the death of their loved ones. She explains to them that death has cleaved the surviving partner in half, and one would not expect a person who has that kind of injury to go back to work in three weeks. Nor would one be expected to go to the grocery store or really to do anything. The surviving spouse needs to give themselves permission to grieve and heal.

"That is the thing about grief," she said, "It is always changing and morphing. It is good to have a curiosity about how this experience will transform you. Permission and forgiveness are my two big buzz words for grief."

The conversations I had with the people in this chapter reinforced that end-of-life doulas are not just "millennial mumbo jumbo." I am hopeful that the concept of using a doula when someone is diagnosed with a terminal illness will become mainstream in the future. We all need help with life's transitions, especially one as emotional and heartbreaking as death.

LESSONS LEARNED ABOUT DOULAS:

- We learn some of the best lessons when life is hard.
- Be a smart death consumer.
- Ask if you are extending life or extending suffering.
- Don't get caught in ordinary time during an extraordinary time.
- Trust your instincts about what is the right end-of-life treatment.
- Respect the wishes of the dying person.
- Regret is a part of grief.

CHAPTER ELEVEN:
JUST BREATHE
Self-Care Before and After a Loss

"YOU DON'T HAVE TO TRY SO HARD,
YOU DON'T HAVE TO GIVE IT ALL AWAY.
YOU JUST HAVE TO GET UP, GET UP, GET UP."
Colbie Caillat

A s a new widow, I am still trying to figure out what "taking care of myself" means. I am taking care of myself by walking several miles every day. I am taking care of myself by staying in close touch with my family and friends.

But then there are those nights when I still cannot sleep, and I still cannot keep from worrying about the future and what it might hold for me as a single woman living alone. What if I get sick or fall and there is no one there to help me?

I have asked friends how they think I am doing. Some of them tell me I am doing great and seem better. Others tell me I do not seem like the same person they knew before my husband died.

All of this has made me wonder what one should do to move forward, stay motivated, and find a new normal. I have thought long and hard about this part of the journey, the long road ahead after you lose a partner.

It has occurred to me that this journey is similar to going on a diet to lose weight. You know you need to lose weight because you will feel better and be healthier. But you keep putting it off. It will take a lot of demanding work to go on that diet, and that is the last thing you want at that moment. So, you keep searching for an easier way to reach your goal, knowing deep inside that you will eventually need to do the demanding work to get there.

Every widow I spoke with mentioned the exhaustion and depression associated with widowhood. Many had been caregivers to their spouses, to the detriment of their own health and well-being.

Self-care is the last thing many of these people thought about, yet it is a critical step in working through grief and loss. It is a hard step because so often, we put others before ourselves, but we cannot move forward on our journey without healing our minds and bodies first.

As I spoke with friends about the issue of self-care, I often heard, "I have a friend who went through this. You should talk with her." Two of those widows, Mary and Kim, were kind enough to speak with me. They have different stories, but both helped me understand what is almost impossible to see when a loved one becomes ill and faces death: You are not only trying to find the strength to care for your loved one, but strength to keep yourself alive and well during that journey.

Mary was the first widow I contacted, and we had a lengthy phone conversation about her experience. Mary told me that she and her husband, Fred, had been happily married for forty-four years when Fred was diagnosed with vascular dementia. Fred was very sanguine about his diagnosis; his father had died at age fifty-nine, so Fred assumed he would also die at an early age. The fact that he had lived to age eighty, and had lived a wonderful life, gave him peace with the diagnosis. Mary and Fred put their affairs in order and prepared to meet his end with as much dignity as possible.

Mary took charge of Fred's care, typical for her type A personality. For three years, she was his companion, cook, and nurse. She set up a hospital bed in their living room and slept nearby so she could address his needs 24/7. "There were times Fred would call out for me in the early hours of the morning, and I would have to pause and take a deep breath," she recalled, "and then I would tell myself, 'Mary, you can do this.'" Mary did not get a full night of uninterrupted sleep for months.

Both Fred and Mary were determined not to dwell on Fred's impending death or how Mary would cope after he was gone. One night, they discussed just how scared they both were, holding each other as they cried about their fate. After that night, they pledged to adopt a more optimistic outlook and live the rest of their days together as best they could.

Fred's condition worsened over time, and Mary became physically exhausted. Finally, a few months before he died, Mary hired someone to help her in the afternoons, so she had some respite. Still, she was tending to him every morning and up with him every night.

When a hospice worker told Mary that Fred's life was ending, she arranged for him to die in the manner he wished—with her and their dog, Cooper, by his side. She said that is how he wanted to end his days, and that is exactly what happened.

Mary was strong in the days after Fred died and held up during the funeral. But the years of caring for Fred finally caught up with her. Three weeks after Fred's funeral, Mary was hospitalized with bleeding ulcers and diverticulitis. Mary ended up in the hospital four times in the next twelve months; she was physically and emotionally spent.

Mary has since regained her health and, upon reflection, realizes that she should have asked for help long before she did. She remembers that one of the hospice nurses commented, "You're trying to be his nurse and his wife. If you ask for more help, you can focus on being his wife." Mary told me she didn't heed the nurse's advice because Fred was such a private person; she knew that he would not want anyone else tending to his personal needs.

Mary also fell into the trap that so many caregivers do—she thought she was the only person who could provide the right care. She did not realize that in providing that care, she was extending herself far beyond her capabilities, both physically and emotionally. Many of her friends advised her to get more help, but she ignored that advice.

At the beginning of her second year of widowhood, Mary decided to join a grief group to help her grapple with her emotions. The people in the group were at various stages in their grief journey: some were newly widowed, like Mary, and some had been widowed for a few years. A couple of people told her, "If you think year two is bad, wait until year three."

Mary thought that could not be true. But today, she is in year three and found that is the case. She has come to the realization that her situation is not going to change—she will never be able to fix Fred's absence or make it better. After forty-seven years of marriage, the hole left by his absence will always be with her.

Mary is moving along with life. When Cooper died a few months ago, she decided she did not want to rattle around her big house alone, so she signed up to get another puppy. Her successful marriage has made Mary long for another companion, so she took another bold step—she enrolled on Match.com. At age seventy-five, she is not ready to give up on having a relationship and believes there are men out there who are in the same position. She does not know where that journey will take her, but she is determined to try it.

Mary's advice to women caring for an ill husband is to be a wife and not a nurse. She urges everyone who is tackling caregiving duties by themselves to get caregiving assistance sooner rather than later. "I was a nurse, and now I'm not even sure that was what Fred wanted," she said. "I wish I had more time with him as his wife."

She also encourages people to join a grief group to help them shine a light on their emotions and express how they feel. Mary said she was so ill the first year after Fred's death that she did not really have an opportunity to process what she was going through, and it came back to haunt her. "The mental adjustment from wife to widow is enormous and should not be glossed over."

There were a lot of lessons learned in listening to Mary's story. I know that I didn't take the best care of myself during Bucky's illness and I was reluctant to bring in any help beyond family. As I've noted, I also didn't get counseling to help me grapple with the emotions associated with being a new widow. I was stuck, and remained stuck, for a long time after Bucky died.

It is hard to know how to move on after such a loss. To better understand how surviving spouses can care for themselves, I sought the perspective of a psychologist I have known for years, Nancy Van Dyken. Nancy is the founder of Healing Relationships, as well as the author of many books aimed at helping people resolve conflict and deal with depression and anxiety. In her practice, she helps people heal relationships of all kinds—including their relationships with themselves.

I spoke with Nancy about my own experience and those of the widows I had interviewed. She confirmed that some people exhaust themselves caring for a dying spouse, only to realize after their spouses' deaths that they spent too little time caring for themselves. She said people often are in shock, preoccupied with figuring out the next steps. Denial also plays a big part, and she told me that it's very hard to take care of ourselves when we're in denial. She reiterated what I already knew—a lot of people wait and wait for their situations to get better, and, of course, most often, they do not.

DON'T GET STUCK IN GRIEF

I learned from Nancy that the general rule of thumb is that it takes about four years to process the loss of a parent and about seven years for the loss of a child. But when people have been married for a long time and have a close bond, it takes a long, long time to come to terms with that loss. She said there is no easy way to predict when someone will come out the other side of grief.

She explains to her clients that they can either accept grief or spend the rest of their lives avoiding grief. The only guarantee in this process is pain, and they will either learn to walk through it or they won't. She told me some people get stuck in their grief, and then they get stuck feeling like a victim.

She related a story that exemplified that point. A woman in Nancy's neighborhood had an eighteen-year-old son who died in the shower. The woman was understandably angry about his death and was determined to sue the fire department medics for not reviving him. She didn't understand that, by law, medics cannot attempt resuscitation when a person is already dead. Next, she sued the hospital for not properly diagnosing her son when he was there just prior to his death.

The woman was so full of anger that she could only focus on revenge. She could not accept that her son's death was beyond her control and that she needed to let her anger go and move on to a place of acceptance of what she could not change. Nancy said that people like her neighbor, who get stuck in victim mode, often aren't able to move on past their grief.

Nancy told me another problem she sees is when people try to control things—like a terminal medical diagnosis—that can't be controlled. She said that is a mistake because there is a lot of healing that can happen when someone lets go of their desire to control a situation and just trusts that everything will be OK. She advises that even when we don't know how things will turn out, the ability to get to a place of spirituality or faith can bring solace.

HOW TO GET UNSTUCK

I spoke to Nancy about my feeling of exhaustion and being stuck in grief. She explained that when people are grieving, they are often also depressed, and that slows down their energy. The energy field around someone in grief moves very sluggishly. Her guidance on one way to overcome it is to physically move. She said exercise can help alleviate that malaise, be it walking, biking, or yoga, whatever the person chooses to do. She said movement distributes energy around the body, which then helps to transition from sluggishness and depression to having more energy and less depression.

Nancy also encourages grieving clients to do some creative work, from knitting or working in the garden to writing or painting. She said creativity works in much the same way as physical activity—it moves energy. She recommends that people do something they enjoy, even if it's only for twenty minutes a day. This creativity, she said, also helps people get unstuck.

FULFILL YOUR LIFELONG DREAMS

Nancy ended our conversation by providing concrete examples of how to move forward after the death of a spouse. She said most of us have dreams of something we would like to pursue, whether that is travel, further education, or focusing on a hobby. So, one way she suggests overcoming grief is to pursue a lifelong dream. She said, "Think about Dr. Seuss. He didn't start writing until late in life. Michelangelo's greatest works came after he turned fifty."

She pointed out that when we are younger, and even through middle age, we can be consumed by family or professional obligations. Those activities and obligations often don't allow time for us to pursue our own interests. Nancy encourages older people who have been widowed to create a new life by finding their passion and spending time doing all the things they never had time to do earlier in life.

I found my discussion with Nancy to be helpful and practical. She helped me understand that my feelings of being stuck are normal, yet also helped me realize that I need to find a purpose to move forward.

Kim was the second widow I was referred to, and I discovered that she not only found her own purpose but a way in which to help other widows.

Kim told me that her life was forever altered when her husband, Mark, was diagnosed with glioblastoma, a brain cancer for which there is no cure. Kim had always thought of widows as little old ladies, but now she realized she was going to join their ranks at the age of forty-four.

Kim had to grapple with the prospect of raising their two sons, ages eight and ten, alone, while Mark wrestled with the knowledge he was going to die. He listened to the doctor's advice and then weighed his options. He chose to undergo surgery and chemotherapy so he could extend the time he had with Kim and the boys.

Kim said that raising her children as a single mother was not her only concern; Mark was self-employed, so there was no automatic paycheck coming each month. His business specialized in manufacturing and selling chemicals to the metal processing and finishing industry, something Kim knew little about. When Mark could no longer work, Kim was left to run the business. She told me she felt overwhelmed, but Mark wrote extensive notes about the formulas and other important aspects of the business so Kim could step up to the challenge.

Kim said she quickly learned the technical aspects of the business and became an adept salesperson. In time, running the company turned out to be beneficial. Kim was her own boss and could set her own hours, which gave her the flexibility she needed to care for Mark and be at home with her sons when she needed to be.

Kim told me Mark lived for a year after his diagnosis. Near the end, he was kept alive by a feeding tube. Fortunately, Mark had an advance directive in place, specifying that he did not want to be kept alive by artificial means. She knew that as Mark's advocate, her role was to do what he would have wanted because he was not able to speak for himself. Kim had to make the difficult decision to bring Mark home with hospice care.

But after she settled Mark in at home, Kim said she questioned whether she had made the right decision to remove his feeding tube. Finally, a hospice nurse told her, "You did the right thing by bringing him home. And the feeding tube is not feeding him; it's feeding the tumor." The assurance from the nurse reinforced Kim's instincts that she had done the right thing, at the right time, for Mark. Mark was able to die peacefully at home.

Kim went through the difficulties familiar to most widows. She said it was hard to manage everything on her own. She said she and Mark had been a team. They had no assigned tasks around the house; they each took care of what needed to be done. She told me he would even bake cookies or sew on buttons if needed. Kim and Mark managed their money together, so Kim understood their finances and had a list of their passwords. She knows that compared to many widows, she had a leg up in that respect.

Still, Kim found it hard to manage everything after Mark died. She closed accounts, contacted the credit bureaus, consolidated bank accounts, called the Social Security Administration, changed their insurance, and dealt with the tax filings. Kim told me she was proud that she was keeping their business going, but selling chemicals was not her passion.

As she worked through all of the issues settling Mark's estate and creating her own accounts, an idea came to her about combining her newfound knowledge of estate and financial documents with her skills as a writer.

Kim reflected that for the first year after Mark died, she kept detailed notes and file folders for everything. She wondered how widows who do not have her experience in managing a household cope with these tasks after the death of their spouses. She thought, "What if they have never written a check or do not know account numbers?"

THE BEGINNING OF WIDOW 411

It was an "aha" moment for Kim. She said she knew she had the skills and knowledge to help other widows grapple with these tasks, so she started work on a website that would do just that. She launched the website *Widow 411,* a site that contains resources focused on grief, money, self-care, and all the mundane issues that can overwhelm someone who has lost a spouse. She chose to include 411 in the name because that is the number to call for information.

Kim said she has also created an online course to help people understand income and expenses and what to do with a mortgage or life insurance. She said some people do not even know if they have life insurance, so she provides information in the online course on how to find a policy.

Kim realizes that it can be overwhelming to assume responsibility for all of these tasks, so she approaches it from the standpoint that a reader has no knowledge and then takes them through how to handle things on a step-by-step basis. She provides checklists, as well as templates and worksheets to guide someone through settling their personal affairs. For example, there is a template of a letter to send to a credit card company to close an account or to send to a harassing debt collector.

Kim told me she has also done extensive research on Social Security survivor benefits. She said it is common for widows to get incorrect information from the Social Security Administration, so it is important to understand how the calculations are determined so they can detect a discrepancy. She emphasized that it is critical to know what questions to ask so widows are not blindly accepting the information they receive.

I commented to Kim that she had more than a full plate. I asked how she was able to care for herself during this time. She admitted that self-care was something she overlooked for a long time.

MAKE YOURSELF THE PRIORITY

Kim told me that working on the website helped her work through her grief, but still, she suffered mentally and physically. In the first few years after Mark died, she did not take care of herself because her focus was on caring for her boys and running the business.

But eventually, her body began to show signs of stress. She had persistent pain in her neck for almost four years. She knew there was a place near her that offered monthly memberships for massages. She decided that if she signed up and the massage was being charged to her credit card every month that she would be forced to make an appointment and go.

She said, looking back, it sounds ridiculous to say she had to force herself to get a massage every month, but she did. She knew that she was so stressed and tense that she needed that massage. Still, she told me she grappled with thinking it was too indulgent to be focusing on herself.

Now that she has worked with so many widows, she has observed that some widows don't know how to help themselves because they are so deep in their grief. Other widows think they need to rely on other people to help them. Kim likes to remind widows that no one is coming to save them—they must learn to save themselves.

She has also seen some widows who are convinced that nothing will ever be good again, and Kim is not sure those people can be helped. She said they must want to be better—happier—and there are ways they can do that, but they must be willing to make themselves a priority.

Kim acknowledged that it is not easy to prioritize yourself after a death because everything is so overwhelming and stressful. But everyone needs to figure out what self-care means to them and then do something about it. For her, it was monthly massages and an occasional pedicure.

ASK FOR HELP

I asked Kim if, like me, she had avoided therapy after Mark died. She said that in the immediate aftermath of his death, she was too consumed with family and their business to think about her own mental health. She eventually went to therapy four years after Mark died. She learned that therapy is another form of self-care and a way to help find a support system.

She now advises widows that when people ask what they need, to tell them. Kim said asking for help is self-care. She feels this is so important that she has devoted a section in her guide on ways in which to help widows. Kim suggests to every widow that they make a list of what they need, and when someone asks how they can help, give them a task from that list. It can be cleaning leaves out of the gutter or taking out the trash.

CHOOSE HOW YOU WANT TO LIVE

I thought Kim's approach to her own situation was an excellent example of how widows can turn something bad into something positive. Sometimes it can be personal, and sometimes it can be to help others, as Kim has chosen to do. I asked her how she has coped so well with all that was thrown at her.

She told me her philosophy is that circumstances do not happen *to* us; they just happen. She said, "People have the option to choose their thoughts, choose how to live, and choose how not to live. Some widows are angered or upset by something a friend has said or done. I tell them that no one can make them feel a certain way. A friend cannot make them happy or sad without their consent."

She has seen that grief can do powerful things to our brains and make us more sensitive. She said when we're grieving, we expect that people should be a certain way or act a certain way. But our grief is not the other person's experience. So, she tells widows who are feeling slighted or hurt that it is unrealistic to expect their friends to understand grief when they have had no experience with it.

Kim pointed out that a new widow is inexperienced with grief herself, so there is no roadmap for how everyone should act. She believes that frequently our frustration or anger at someone else reflects our own insecurities about whether we are managing things in the right way.

Kim told me she had the same experience I did: She did not recognize herself for a long time because she was not the same person she used to be. She feels that the loss of a spouse is very different than other losses. When a spouse dies, the surviving spouse loses their identity, income, friendships, their whole way of living. That is vastly different from losing a grandparent or friend. In her experience, Kim has seen for herself and with other widows that nothing compares to the loss of a spouse, and the secondary losses that go with it. People who lose a spouse experience the most devastating, stressful life event.

A LIGHT AT THE END OF THE TUNNEL

Finally, Kim and I spoke about her journey from overwhelmed widow to someone who is moving on with life. She told me it has now been seven years since Mark died, and she feels she has come out the other end of grief. She admits that she was very scared the first few years after Mark died, when she was learning to run the business and trying to shepherd her sons through their own grief.

She said that at the time, there was a lot going on, and it was almost impossible to see an eventual destination. But she kept an open mind and would tell herself that although things were not good, they would get better. She said that was her mantra.

Kim said that coming through grief was certainly not all smooth sailing. As a family, they had some rough years, but they are all coming out the other side. She said they have learned a lot and are all moving forward, and that is a good thing.

Kim told me she is getting remarried. She knows that is not a choice all widows make, but it is a good thing for her.

She remains focused on helping other widows. She said, "I am not the widow whisperer. I do not have everything figured out; I am still figuring it out as I go." But her goal is to continue to share information when she does figure something out.

She encourages widows by telling them that there is a light at the end of the tunnel; things do get better, but it takes time. She said what that means is different for everyone, but to get better, you must believe that it is possible. The universe works in mysterious ways, and you must be open to it.

I was so inspired after my discussions with the women in this chapter. It is hard to explain to anyone who is not a widow what it feels like to be stuck in grief. When you are stuck, the last thing you care about is taking care of yourself. It almost feels like a betrayal to your spouse to make plans for the future or take part in activities that are new and broadening. But, in fact, that is what we all must do to move onward with our lives. It is not easy, but it is another necessary step to coming out the other side of grief.

LESSONS LEARNED ABOUT SELF-CARE:

- Don't ignore self-care. Make yourself and your well-being a priority.

- Acting as a victim can keep you stuck in grief.

- Don't be afraid to ask friends and family for help. Make a list of things you need done, and use that list for suggestions when people ask how they can help.

- The loss of a spouse is the most life-altering loss one can endure. It is important to find a new normal to move forward.

- Fulfill lifelong dreams—travel, learn new hobbies, take classes, whatever you have ever dreamed of doing.

CHAPTER TWELVE: BUILDING A NEW BEGINNING

The Relief of Finding Meaningful Focus

"I'LL COME FLYING THROUGH YOUR DOOR,
AND YOU'LL KNOW WHAT LOVE IS FOR."
Paul McCartney

EVERY DAY IN the three years since Bucky passed away, I've asked myself: "How are you doing today?" I am not waiting for my grief to pass, because I know it will always be there. It will not be as bad as it was the first week, or the first month, or the first year, but it will stay with me until the day I die.

The death of a spouse changes you. It changes the way you look at life. There have been days when I wondered if I would ever feel like my old self. I do believe you can find happiness again, but it is a different kind of happiness.

I have talked with other widows whose lives are rich with friends and family. They have discovered new interests and hobbies since their spouse died, and in some cases, they have found someone new to love.

Two people I interviewed, Melanie Bloom and Ron Rudolph, exemplify the ability to come through grief and subsequently use their loss to bring light to others,

I was introduced to Melanie by Lee Woodruff. They were long-time friends, and Lee thought Melanie might be a good person to provide perspective on finding meaning after the death of a spouse.

Melanie and I spoke at length about her journey through grief and how she came through it. Melanie suffered the loss of her husband, David, in a very public manner. David was an embedded correspondent for NBC News during the Iraq war, so his death was a loss she shared with millions of viewers. Melanie found a way to move forward and honor David through educating others about the disease that killed him. In doing so, she turned his public death into a public service.

Melanie and David's story began in Wichita, Kansas. They were living in the same apartment complex, so Melanie describes him as "literally the boy next door." They dated for two years before marrying in 1990.

David's intelligence, rapier wit, and boyish good looks made him a rising star at NBC, and the couple began a life on the move. His career took them from Wichita to Miami, then to Chicago and Los Angeles. In Washington, D.C., he became the White House correspondent, an assignment that can make or break a career. David thrived. Not only did he remain popular among his peers, but when he left that job, President Clinton commented that David's "integrity and good humor will be missed." David's final post was in New York, where, among other assignments, he anchored the weekend edition of *The Today Show*.

In 2003, when the war in Iraq was new and hope for progress prevailed, journalists jockeyed for front-line assignments embedded with the troops. NBC selected David to be its reporter on the ground. He was attached to the Third Infantry Division, where he became a much-liked companion, just another member of the tight-knit team. So much so, that the division eventually retrofitted a flatbed truck for him, outfitted with live television and satellite transmission equipment. Dubbed the "Bloom-mobile," it allowed David to broadcast his reports as the division made its way toward Baghdad.

Melanie was nervous about David's dangerous assignment. She watched his reporting on TV with her heart in her throat. She developed a new appreciation for what military spouses go through when their loved ones are deployed to distant lands.

David sent letters home and wrote a lot about the troops—or "his guys," as he referred to them. Whenever he sent emails to Melanie and his daughters, he asked them to not only pray for him but for all the men and women, mothers and fathers, who were with him. He had a true affinity for the people he worked with and reported on.

David became a familiar face to people back in the US as he reported tirelessly on the progress of the troops. He got little sleep, and the space in the Bloom-mobile was cramped and hot. One night, as he made a phone call to Melanie, his legs were cramping so badly that he risked climbing out of the truck, exposing himself to potential hostile fire.

Those pains in his legs turned out to be more than leg cramps. Tragically, on April 6, 2003, David died because of a blood clot that formed in his leg. The clot traveled to an artery in his lungs, causing a fatal pulmonary embolism. The diagnosis was deep vein thrombosis, caused by the countless hours of sitting in the cramped space of the Bloom-mobile. This affable reporter, who was so talented and well-liked, died at the age of thirty-nine. Back home, Melanie was caring for their nine-year-old twin daughters, Christine and Nicole, and their three-year-old daughter, Ava, unaware that she had joined the ranks of Iraq war widows.

The night of April 6, Melanie's phone rang in the middle of the night, and she was informed that David had died. For a long time after that, Melanie was sure every time the phone rang that it would be David on the other end. When she turned on the news at night, she would wait to see him come on the screen. She waited for him to walk in the door and tell her this was all just a big mistake. It was a long time before she truly felt his absence and knew that it was permanent. Even today, if she receives a phone call in the middle of the night, her heart begins to beat rapidly, and she suffers from PTSD. She has asked her friends never to call at night.

She said David's death felt like an amputation, where a limb is no longer there but phantom pain persists. He was gone, but she still felt his presence. All the plans they had made for the future remained in her head, and those plans did not die suddenly because David had passed away.

As Melanie was processing the news of David's death, her thoughts turned to the letters he had written to her in the weeks prior to his death. Specifically, she focused on his request to have her think about and pray for all the others he was with. Melanie had a newfound appreciation for the grief all people experience when they lose a loved one, regardless of the circumstances.

Melanie also had a looming problem: How was she going to support the family? She had not worked in years due to their frequent moves and caring for three small children. David's career had supplied the paycheck for their family, and that came to an abrupt halt when he died. Suddenly, she had to figure out how she could provide for herself and the girls.

Melanie and David had made the same mistake so many young couples do; they had not prepared for a death. They did not have wills or powers of attorney. After David's funeral, a lot of their friends and family vowed to make wills and get their affairs in order, so Melanie knows that some good came out of their situation. She now advises young people to plan for the worst and hope for the best.

For the first year after David's death, Melanie said she tended to pain: her own, and more importantly, that of her girls. She asked herself, "How do I pull myself out of this abyss of grief?" She put one foot in front of the other, trying to bring some sense of normalcy back into the children's lives to eke out a bit of joy. She wanted to model behavior for her daughters to help them move forward; the girls were looking to her for how they should act and cope with their grief. She said, "It was important to find a way to laugh and to live the life their dad would have wanted them to have."

Melanie sought advice on how to best help her children through grief. Her first act had been to seek counsel from her priest on how to break the news of David's death to them. He told her to tell them immediately, not to engage in a long, drawn-out beginning, but to begin with, "Your daddy has died," and then move on to the rest. The girls reacted just as Melanie had at first, with disbelief. They asked her if he was sick and if they could visit him in a hospital. One of her twins had a myriad of questions, while the other just wept and was silent. Melanie was committed to honoring their individual paths through grief.

Melanie's youngest daughter, Ava, had been a happy baby and a chatterbox before David died. But after his death, she stopped talking and eating and barely slept. Watching Ava suffer was agonizing, second only to losing David.

Melanie learned from a therapist that age three is generally when a little girl falls in love with her dad. Ava was smack in the middle of that when David died. Finally, more than seven months after David's passing, Melanie received a phone call from Ava's preschool to tell her that Ava had spoken. Melanie cites her relief in receiving that phone call as a giant step toward moving on.

As Melanie worked through her grief, she began to read the thousands of letters she received from the public. She was touched by their outreach and expressions of sympathy, each telling her how much David had meant to them. But something else began to emerge from the correspondence: People credited David with saving their lives. Deep vein thrombosis (DVT) has some specific symptoms, but they are often overlooked or dismissed. Many people had not heard about DVT until it took David's life. After news reporters talked about his symptoms on TV, many viewers visited their doctors and got an early diagnosis.

Just as Katie Couric brought attention to colon cancer after the death of her spouse, Melanie began to raise awareness about DVT. David had complained of leg cramps two days before he died, and Melanie is convinced that if they had known the symptoms, his life could have been saved. Her mission became educating others about DVT so no one else would have to die from it.

Helping others, and doing so in David's memory, helped Melanie realize that David's death was not in vain. She also believed her work with DVT awareness modeled behavior to her daughters that signaled they could take this large loss and do something with it—to find a positive out of such a negative. For fifteen years, Melanie went on media circuits and gave speeches about DVT. Her efforts to help others provided her a feeling of purpose and healing.

Melanie settled into her role as a single mother and DVT advocate. She lived by the motto "Where there is life, there is hope." She held onto her hope. She had her life, her girls, close family, and friends. That was a lot of life for her. She focused on being happy. David had sought joy and passion in everything he did, and she knew he would want that for Melanie and the girls.

Melanie told me that remarriage was not a goal. She lived by the adage "Better to have loved and lost than never to have loved at all." But three years after David's death, friends encouraged her to date again. Reluctantly, she did. Two years later, she met a wonderful man, Daniel, who was a widower raising two children.

Melanie and Daniel eventually married, creating a large, blended family. Today, her daughters are all doing well. They know they will live with the loss of their father for life, but they have learned to accept its ups and downs. There are times, such as father-daughter dances, proms, and graduations, when they feel the loss more acutely. Those are also the occasions when Melanie reflects on how David was robbed of sharing them. But in general, Melanie feels they have all come through to the "other side" of their grief.

Melanie encourages her friends, whether widowed or divorced, to open themselves up to new experiences and new love. She tells them, "Honor your struggle, but once you've done that, look around because there's a lot of life and a lot of love out there. Be open to it."

Ron Rudolph is a man who was open to change in an entirely different way. I came across his story while reading about widowed people, and when I contacted him about an interview, he was happy to oblige. Ron is someone who might give us all hope. Through the tragic death of his wife, he found purpose, meaning, and a way to move forward with a renewed spirit, all inspired by his late wife's love of a bluebird.

Ron said he and his wife, Pat, were on vacation, taking a leisurely stroll when Pat suddenly became dizzy and unable to continue. They immediately sought medical attention, assuming it was something minor. But further testing revealed that the breast cancer that Pat had beaten back years before had returned. Now it had metastasized to her brain.

Both Ron and Pat were shocked. They thought that cancer was behind them. Ron was close to retirement after working forty-five years in the specialty shop at a lumber company. They were excited about the plans they had made for the next chapter in their lives. Suddenly, that future was uncertain.

Ron made sure Pat was comfortable at home and became her primary caregiver. Family and friends pitched in to help when he was at work. Ron said it became painfully obvious where Pat's condition was headed. The doctors told him what to expect, but they never said how long she had to live. The doctors routinely explained the progressive symptoms of the disease to Ron, and each time, shortly after their discussions, Pat would experience those symptoms.

Eventually, Ron arranged to have part-time help come to their home to care for Pat, but over time it was clear that she required full-time professional care. Ron placed Pat in a hospice home, Our Lady of Peace, where she passed away eighteen months after her diagnosis.

Ron said he tried to prepare himself for Pat's death but found that no amount of forethought could brace him for the shock of losing his wife of thirty-eight years. After Pat died, Ron received support from family and friends, but within days everyone went home, and he was alone in their house. A week after the funeral, he awakened in the middle of the night, suffering from an anxiety attack. He felt like he could not breathe, and he began to wonder how he would ever get through the grieving process.

Sleep was elusive, so at two o'clock in the morning, he got out of bed. It was a freezing January night in Minnesota; nevertheless, Ron dressed and headed outside to his workshop.

He walked in the door, flipped on the lights, and his eyes landed on a bluebird house hanging on the wall. Pat had loved watching bluebirds, so Ron had built bluebird houses for her and placed them around the yard. That night he decided the best way to relieve his anxiety was to build more birdhouses. He started sawing pieces of wood and assembling them. By the time the sun came that morning, Ron had crafted eight birdhouses.

Later that day, he called his daughter, Kristy, to see if she could help him distribute them. She said, "Dad, it's January in Minnesota. Who wants a birdhouse?"

Still, Kristy went onto Facebook Marketplace and told his story. A few days later, she called Ron and said, "Dad, I think we're going to need more birdhouses."

Ron went from building birdhouses in his spare time to running a full-time birdhouse business. He learned everything he could about boxing and shipping his product. Working with his hands on something dear to Pat gave him purpose and kept him busy during a painful, life-shattering time. The Facebook business boomed, and demand was so great that he recruited his ninety-year-old father and his grandsons to help. His hobby had become a four-generation business.

The Rudolph's Bluebird Houses page soon caught the attention of the people at Facebook. Ron and Kristy were invited to Facebook headquarters in Menlo Park, California, for media day.

Facebook was intrigued by Ron's story—they never imagined that someone would use their platform to deal with loss. At the conference, Ron was seated next to a woman who introduced herself, saying, "Hi, I'm Cheryl Sandberg."

Ron turned to Kristy and asked, "Who is Cheryl Sandberg?"

When he learned that he was seated beside the chief operating officer of the world's largest online social network, he hesitated but then told Cheryl his story. In turn, Cheryl gave Ron *Plan B,* the book she wrote about losing her husband.

After that, media requests came in, including an appearance on *The Today Show.* Ron began to hear from a lot of people who had also suffered a loss, and he realized that his story was helping others. But while he was happy assisting others, he knew that he still needed help for his grief.

He enrolled in a grief counseling session but was quickly turned off by it. The first session involved "introducing" their spouse to the group. Ron said he just could not do it. He went home and vowed never to go back. But when he called the counselor to give her that news, she encouraged him to give it another try. Ron knew that his eight grandchildren were watching him, and he did not want them to see him continue to mope. So, he signed up for the next session.

Ron said he is never late for anything, but when he drove to the meeting place, he remained in his car as the other members of the group entered the building. He doubted if they were going through what he was going through. Finally, he walked in late and sat down with his arms and legs crossed, convinced this group was not going to help him.

When it came time for Ron to speak, he introduced himself and told his story. Then he listened to others tell their stories. Slowly, Ron began to see that everyone in the room was on a level playing field; everyone had experienced the same painful grief as him. He felt their compassion for him, and in return, he felt compassion for them. He had not thought that was possible.

Ron learned that men usually shy away from grief therapy. He acknowledges that he was one of those reluctant men, but now believes that everyone should be open to receiving help.

"Men and women alike suffer grief, and it's important to know what to do with it when it comes," he told me. "That's where counseling really helps. I was thinking, 'I'm a man, and I don't need help,' but what a bunch of BS that was. It was the best thing I did."

Ron's grief group yielded another bonus: He met his new wife, Kathleen, at one of the meetings. When the sessions ended after eight weeks, the members exchanged phone numbers so they could continue to talk or get together. Kathleen contacted Ron. She had seen his bluebird houses on Facebook and wanted to buy one.

They met for coffee and ended up talking for hours. They were the same age, had the same number of children and even their grandchildren were the same ages. They had both lost spouses, so they understood what the other had experienced.

Ron and Kathleen married in October 2020. It was a small ceremony, with only their close family members in attendance, due to the COVID-19 restrictions in their city.

Ron and Kathleen are incredibly happy. "We talk about our spouses. It is not a subject we avoid because they will always be with us. Nobody is trying to replace anybody, and we acknowledge what has happened."

Ron's birdhouse business is still flourishing, and the success of his efforts now benefits others. Ron decided early on that he would donate any profits he made from the business to a worthy cause.

He started the business to remember and honor Pat, and he wanted any money he made to continue that mission. He thought back to the days when Pat was so ill, when he had to hire in-home help that cost $300 per day. He had paid that amount for the first month but quickly realized that although he had money in savings, it was not enough to sustain that kind of expense. When Pat entered Our Lady of Peace hospice care, they accepted her free of charge.

"When she was able to go to the hospice home, I felt guilty for feeling so good about that," Ron said. "I felt like a weight had been lifted off me. There were so many things I was trying to deal with: emotions, finances, my job, and losing my wife. When they called and said she could stay there, it allowed me to go back to being a husband. I no longer had to be all the other things she needed."

So, to honor Pat and give back to Our Lady of Peace, Ron donates his profits to them each year on Pat's birthday. At last count, he had made over 5,500 birdhouses and now offers how-to birdhouse building classes to youth groups, daycares, church groups, and care centers.

"Everybody's good at something," he told me. "Everybody's got a hobby or a passion. I encourage everyone to draw on their talent and use it."

AFTERWORD

I WAS SHOCKED WHEN I experienced so many problems after Bucky died. I had not anticipated any of them.

I was certain I could not be the only widow who had stumbled down this road, and that certainty became the impetus for this book. I wanted to help other women avoid the pitfalls so many widows encounter.

But as I spoke with widows and the professionals who helped them, I realized that the information I gathered was applicable to anyone who is going to die or has a loved one who is going to die. That happens to be 100 percent of us. I was amazed by the number of people who had not given any thought to their estate plan or what they wanted their legacy to be. It should not have been all that surprising since Bucky and I were certainly in that category.

Bucky and I did not have all our documents in place, nor did we have some important conversations. I am still trying to decide where to spread his ashes. It is something we never discussed, and now I feel guilty that I do not know what he would want me to do with them. I feel as if he would like to be free from the urn I keep locked away in the house, but I am unsure about how, where, and when to free him.

Writing this book made me take a hard look at my own estate plan. I have now made sure that my will and trust clearly define what I want for my two daughters. I have written an intention letter, and I have documented where and to whom I want my personal possessions to go. This has given me some peace of mind.

Over the past two years of my research, friends have asked me what I was learning from my interviews. I would tell them stories about people who had not prepared for a death or relate some of the practical advice I had received from professionals. Invariably, they would later tell me they had changed their wills and trusts, or explained their wishes to their spouse, or talked to their children about finances and inheritances. These discussions also reminded people to write down their passwords or to compile all their essential information in a binder. In other words, they prepared and ensured that their families would have vital information in case they did not come home one night.

Now the issue I face is more personal: How do I move on? When the death of a loved one shatters your world, you are left with a painful and uniquely formidable task. You need to start picking up the pieces and figure out where they belong in your changed world.

Friends have told me to try to be happy. I have always considered myself to be happy and lucky and blessed in my life. Of course, there have been trying and challenging times, but none of those experiences ever made me unhappy.

But for months after Bucky's death, I did not recognize myself. The woman I stared at in the mirror looked familiar but was not the same woman who used to jump out of bed every morning ready to take on the day. I was unsure if I would ever be happy or have hope again. I wondered whether I had a form of post-traumatic stress that would be with me for the rest of my life.

I am slowly becoming stronger as I work through my grief. I have learned that the only thing I need to do is be open to whatever lies ahead. I really do not have a choice about going forward because, as the saying goes, "Life goes on."

What I learned in writing this book has changed my life. When we lose a loved one, we can worry and fret our lives away, or we can build a birdhouse.

I have learned that we need to acknowledge that we are living a new life in a new world.

The challenge is to make it our own.

ACKNOWLEDGMENTS

T HERE ARE MANY people who helped make this book possible. First and foremost, I am indebted to the widows who agreed to tell me their stories. It is not easy to open up about the subject of grief and loss. And, for many who talked to me, it was almost like tearing the scab off a healing wound. There were interviews I cried through, and interviews I cried about later, but each and every story taught me a lesson about life, love, and loss.

I am grateful to the professionals who so generously provided their expert advice and guidance on how to navigate the rough waters of widowhood. Their wisdom has made this book a useful resource for anyone facing life alone.

To my friend, Suzanne Sparrow Watson, who believed in this book and agreed to help me write it. She was with me the day Bucky died and has been with me every step along the way. She threw herself into this project from the very beginning.

To my family and my friends, who encouraged and inspired me to keep going and insisted that what I was doing was going to make a difference for other people.

To Kerri Westenberg, who suffered through many Zoom meetings helping edit and create the final version of this book. And to Harvey Mackay, who promised to help me, and who did help me.

I also want to thank Bob Parsons. I am so blessed to have this Vietnam veteran and United States Marine as a friend. He has helped me keep my head above water since the day my husband was diagnosed with cancer. Bob has had my back, and I will be forever grateful to him for that and for so many other kindnesses.

And finally, I want to thank my late husband Bucky for the wonderful life we shared and for the lessons he taught me about courage in the face of death. I hope I make him as proud as he made me on the day it is my turn to say goodbye to all the people I love.

ABOUT THE AUTHORS

Esteemed for her professionalism by viewers, listeners, and her colleagues, the versatile Pat Miles became one of the Minneapolis region's premier television news anchors and radio talk hosts.

After earning her master's degree in journalism at the University of Missouri, Miles worked in both radio and television news in Colorado before joining WCCO TV in 1978 as a reporter and weekend anchor. Her intelligent reporting and authoritative delivery soon brought her to the anchor desk of WCCO's 5:00 PM and 10:00 PM newscasts. She covered every major news event for WCCO TV but was most proud of *A Time to Weep,* her documentary on the famine in Africa. In 1990, she moved to KARE TV, where she anchored the 5:00 PM and 6:00 PM newscasts and developed *A Pat Miles Special,* using her writing and interviewing prowess to tell the stories of notable Minnesotans. When she left TV news in 2001, she fulfilled a lifelong dream by becoming the host of *The Pat Miles Show* weekday mornings on WCCO Radio.

A role model for women in the industry, the Minnesota Broadcasting Hall of Fame member won numerous accolades during her lengthy broadcasting career, including the National Television Academy's Silver Circle Award.

Suzanne Sparrow Watson earned a Bachelor of Arts in History and English Literature. She began her career working for a real estate development company in Fair Oaks, California, writing and designing advertising campaigns. After returning to her native San Francisco Bay Area, she entered the human resources field, working for a commercial insurance company. She was eventually recruited by Bank of America to develop management training programs. Over an eighteen-year career with the bank, she held increasingly responsible positions supporting a wide range of the bank's businesses. She retired in 2002 as Executive Vice President of Human Resources for the Consumer Bank.

In 2004, she wrote her first book, *In the Enemy's Camp*. The book weaves together historical events with the experience of her husband and his family, who endured three and a half years as prisoners in a Japanese internment camp in the Philippines during World War II.

In 2012, she began writing the blog, *From a Bird's Eye View*, which she co-authors with her brother, Bob. Every Monday, they post a short essay about travel, life's little observations, or anything that strikes their fancy—other than politics.

RESOURCES

S EARCHING THE INTERNET for resources or advice can be overwhelming when you are in the midst of caregiving or in the aftermath of the death of a loved one. We have compiled the following recommendations as a useful starting point.

Alzheimer's Association; alz.org
The Alzheimer's Association is the leading non-profit health organization in Alzheimer's care, support, and research. Its website provides information about the disease, resources for care, caregiving support, and volunteer opportunities.

Alzheimers.gov; alzheimers.gov
This website offers information and resources—including tips for caregivers and families—on Alzheimer's disease and related dementias, such as Lewy body dementia, frontotemporal dementia, and vascular dementia. Alzheimers.gov is managed by the National Institute on Aging at the National Institutes of Health, a part of the US Department of Health and Human Services.

American Psychiatric Association; psychiatry.org
This is the primary professional association of psychiatrists in the United States, and its website includes a link to a search for providers.

Brighter Days Grief Center; brighterdaysgriefcenter.org
Brighter Day Grief Center provides free grief support resources, programs, and services for youth, young adults, and adults who are grieving the death or terminal diagnosis of a beloved family member.

International End of Life Doula Association (INELDA); inelda.org
This website, affiliated with NEDA, includes links to informational articles and has a doula directory.

Mayo Clinic Alzheimer's Research Center; mayo.edu/research/centers-programs/alzheimers-disease-research-center
This website offers information on patient care, educational videos, community outreach, publications, and clinical trials.

National End-of-Life Doula Alliance (NEDA); nedalliance.org
NEDA, based in New Hampshire, seeks to inspire positive change in American death practices and provides ethical and practical guidelines to end-of-life doulas. The website has a directory of its members by state.

Soaringspirits.org; soaringspirits.org
Soaring Spirits offers widows a multitude of resources, including new widow packets, regional support groups, an online support group, and Camp Widow.

The Retreat; theretreat.org
In addition to offering residential programs for addiction recovery in Wayzata, Minnesota, The Retreat also offers programs online that can be accessed by individuals anywhere in the world. It also offers a 10-week, peer-based residential program, 55Plus, to help those people trying to get sober in the second half of adult life and are motivated to change and grow.

The 36-Hour Day by Nancy L. Mace, MA, and Peter V. Rabins, MD, MPH
Published by Johns Hopkins Press
This book is an invaluable resource for caregivers of dementia patients. It contains advice for avoiding burnout, plus suggestions for when and how to get additional help. The 2021 edition provides the most up-to-date information on how to hire home care aides, useful apps, promising, preventative techniques and therapies, and much more.

Tragedy Assistance Programs for Survivors (TAPS); taps.org
TAPS provides comfort, care, and resources to those grieving the death of a military loved one, including peer support groups and programming for survivors nationally and worldwide.

What's Your Grief; whatsyourgrief.com
This non-profit organization provides resources related to understanding and coping with grief and loss for people grieving, people helping someone else grieve and grief counselors. It also produces a podcast and a blog.

Widow411; widow411.com
This website offers stories about inspiring widows, tips and classes designed to help guide widows through post-death tasks, and links to other resources.

Wings for Widows; wingsforwidows.org
Wings for Widows is a non-profit organization that provides financial coaching and education for newly widowed women, as well as connections to other widows to lend support and advice.